WHAT THE DOCTORS CAN'T TELL YOU ABOUT

LEVEL 3 AUTISM

I0105687

MODERN DAY PROPHET

Copyright © 2026 By Modern Day Prophet

All Rights Reserved

The front and back covers and all of the
illustrations in this book were designed using

Canva

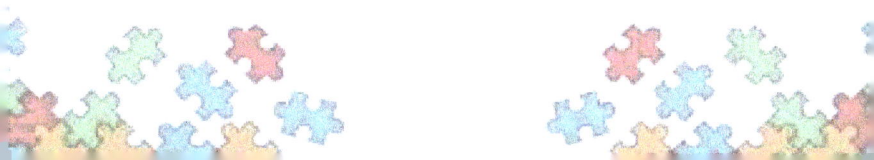

TABLE OF CONTENTS

DEDICATION

I dedicate this book to Cody and Darius, two extraordinary individuals with Level 3 Autism.

WHAT THE DOCTORS CAN'T TELL YOU ABOUT LEVEL 3 AUTISM

FOREWARD

Let me first introduce myself. I am the Modern Day Prophet. Don't pay attention to my name. It just means that I am highly intelligent about various subjects. One subject that I am highly intelligent about is level 3 autism. Level 3 autism may also be known as severe autism or profound autism. I will stick with level 3 autism to avoid any confusion. I will give you a great deal of information about level 3 autism in this book. I will give you information that I know you have never seen before. I will give you information that the doctors and ABA therapists can't give you.

Many of you think that there is something wrong with you and that is why you had a child with level 3 autism. Many of you think that you made a mistake during your pregnancy and that is why you had a child with level 3 autism. Let me dispel these myths. There is nothing wrong with you. You didn't make any mistakes. Autism doesn't come from vaccines or medicines. It doesn't come from bad genetics. It doesn't come from poor health. It doesn't even come from drugs or alcohol. Humans couldn't create the "level 3 autistic condition" if our lives depended on it. Level 3 autism is not even a medical condition. It is a difference. Their brains work differently. Their brains work in a way that no one understands. No one except for me.

I am going to explain level 3 autism in a way that you haven't heard before. I am going to explain it from the perspective of the "creation matrix" or as you may be more familiar with, "Mother Nature". There are certain conditions that people are born with that we as humans have no control over. Some people will be born certain ways and there is nothing that anyone can do about it. There are certain conditions that Mother Nature herself controls. Level 3 autism is one of those conditions. Some people will be born with level 3 autism and others won't. There is nothing that any of us can do about it. Level 3 autism falls directly under the auspices of Mother Nature.

WHAT THE DOCTORS CAN'T TELL YOU ABOUT LEVEL 3 AUTISM

Because of this, Mother Nature will protect her miracles. You didn't have a child with level 3 autism because something was wrong with you. It's the opposite. You had a child because there was something right with you. Mother Nature will only give her miracles to the people who can love, care for, and protect her miracles. If you have a child with level 3 autism it means that you are one of the best parents in the world. You were chosen. You were chosen because you are special.

I am convinced that thousands of years ago people understood level 3 autism much better than we understand it today. I am convinced that people with level 3 autism were utilized much more effectively in society than they are today. I referred to people with level 3 autism as miracles. They are capable of phenomenal things. That's if you understand the advantages that they have. That is one of the problems. People don't understand the advantages.

I said earlier that people with level 3 autism have brains that work differently. They perceive things differently. They understand things differently. They see the world differently. This causes certain challenges and disadvantages for people with level 3 autism. I won't gloss over that fact. There are certain concepts that people with level 3 autism can't process or understand. But Mother Nature didn't leave them high and dry. People with level 3 autism have tremendous advantages to compensate for their disadvantages. People with level 3 autism are capable of phenomenal things. They can do things that the rest of us can't do. No one focuses on their advantages. People only focus on the disadvantages. That's because no one understands the advantages. Not the parents. Not the doctors. Not the ABA therapists.

I believe that Mother Nature is tired of her miracles being mistreated and marginalized. That is why I was given the knowledge and understanding to write this book. If anyone else could have written this book, they would have already done so. No one else in the world has the understanding that I do about level 3 autism. It will be my honor and privilege to share all the

WHAT THE DOCTORS CAN'T TELL YOU ABOUT LEVEL 3 AUTISM

knowledge and information that I have about level 3 autism with all of you. My goal is to improve the quality of life and make the world a better place for all my brothers and sisters. That will only happen if people understand and respect the condition of level 3 autism.

I'm going to tell all of you a secret. Before I wrote this book, I had written a research study. This research study involved virtual reality and level 3 autism. There was a problem. I had no way to get my research study out to anyone. It dawned on me that I had the knowledge and understanding to write a very comprehensive book about level 3 autism. I then wrote this book so that I would have a place to put my research study. Not only are you getting the most comprehensive book in the world about level 3 autism, but you are also getting my research study which is in the last chapter of this book. If you are a parent, doctor, therapist, or someone who takes care of someone with level 3 autism in any way, it is your duty and responsibility to read this book. You will be glad that you did.

WHAT THE DOCTORS CAN'T TELL YOU ABOUT LEVEL 3 AUTISM

CHAPTER 1

IT IS TIME TO TAKE YOUR CHILD OFF THE SPECTRUM

There is something that we need to talk about. We need to talk about this spectrum. This spectrum is commonly known as "autism spectrum disorder". There are three levels to this spectrum. There are levels 1, 2, and 3. Your child is in the level 3 part of the spectrum. There is a difference between level 3 and levels 1 and 2. In the levels 1 and 2 parts of the spectrum there is a vast array of different mental, cognitive, and psychological conditions. In the level 3 part of the spectrum there is only one condition.

This spectrum means that many different neurological and psychological conditions are now considered autism. Asperger's Syndrome, ADHD, schizophrenia, manic depression, and many other conditions are now considered autism. Level 3 autism has been lumped in with a plethora of mental and psychological conditions. What this means is that there are many people who consider themselves autistic and their condition doesn't have anything to do with your child's condition. We are talking about totally different situations. This is why a distinction must be made between your child and these people. How do you think these people on other parts of the spectrum view your child? How do you think that people who aren't on the spectrum view your child? Let's just say that a distinction is being made between the level 3 and levels 1 and 2 parts of the spectrum.

Who do you think is ostracized on the spectrum? Who do you think is marginalized on the spectrum? Who do you think receives the least amount of support on the spectrum? The answer to all three questions is your children. Your children are the ones who are ostracized, marginalized, and ignored. The rest of the spectrum makes sure to distinguish themselves from your children. There is a very good reason for this. The doctors can treat the levels 1 and 2 parts of the spectrum with medicine. They can't treat level 3 with any medications. There is no medicine that can cure level 3 autism. There is no medical procedure that can cure level 3 autism. There is absolutely nothing that the doctors can do about level 3 autism. They don't even understand the condition.

There are many people who consider themselves autistic, but their condition has nothing to do with your child's. We are talking about completely different situations. These people are self-sufficient. Your child is not self-sufficient. These people make sure to let everyone know that they are nothing like your children. They go on their social media and let everyone know that they are autistic, but they are not like your children. They are making the distinction. Now it is time for you to do the same. The time has come for you to disavow the spectrum. The time has come for you to take your kid off the spectrum. The time has come for you to no longer acknowledge this spectrum. They only have your kid on the spectrum to keep them tucked away and invisible. This spectrum hurts people with level 3 autism more than it helps them. You should have figured this out by now. Level 3 autism is not even a medical disability. It is a difference. A difference that no one understands, and that includes the doctors. I can say with absolute certainty that there is no doctor in the world who understands level 3 autism in the way that I do. They don't understand how the brain works in the way that I do. Their PhD's can't help them. You can't learn in school what I know about level 3 autism.

The medical industry has completely fumbled and dropped the ball as it pertains to level 3 autism. Even if there are doctors who understand the difference between an autistic brain and a non-autistic brain, there is no way for them to address the differences. There is nothing in their medical bag of tricks that will help a person with level 3 autism function at a higher level. The truth is that the ball should never have been given to doctors in the first place. Level 3 autism is not a medical issue. It is more of a scientific issue. Level 3 autism fits better under the scientific category than it does in the medical category. Doctors will never be able to further the cause of people with level 3 autism. Scientists may be able to, however. Level 3 autism should be studied and researched as a scientific issue. Scientists will need to study and research logical inputs and logical frequencies.

My goal here is not to disparage doctors. When it comes to your child's overall health and well-being, you definitely want to take them to see a doctor or physician. If your child gets sick or injured, they need to see a doctor. Even for general check-ups. Doctors are very important when it comes to your child's physical health.

WHAT THE DOCTORS CAN'T TELL YOU ABOUT LEVEL 3 AUTISM

They just can't help with your child's level 3 autistic condition. There is no medicine that they can prescribe. There is no medical procedure that they can perform. There is no surgical procedure. There is nothing that a doctor can do to change the way that your child's brain functions. And because these doctors have no real understanding of level 3 autism, they have to way to recognize the advantages that your child possesses.

There are certain challenges that are unique to level 3 autism. I am not downplaying this. There are certain things that people with level 3 autism will never be able to do that non-autistic people will be able to do. What we don't talk about however is that there are things that people with level 3 autism can do that non-autistic people will never be able to do. This is why it is so important to understand these differences.

I want to talk about something very important. There are many misconceptions as to how a person gets level 3 autism. Level 3 autism doesn't come from baby food. It doesn't come from vaccinations. It doesn't come from poor genetics. We are now being told that Tylenol causes level 3 autism in pregnant women, which is ludicrous. There is nothing that we humans can do to create the "level 3 autistic condition". It is beyond our control. The parents didn't do anything wrong. The mother didn't do anything wrong. Some people will acquire level 3 autism and others won't. Some people will be born gay, and others won't. There are certain aspects of creation that we have absolutely no control over. Count level 3 autism among them. In fact, if you have a child with level 3 autism, you can consider yourself a very special person. It is not a coincidence. It is not a coincidence that level 3 autistic children all have the best parents.

Another very important topic that I need to address is medicine. You should never give your level 3 autistic child any medication or drug that will interfere with how their brain functions or attempts to alter the balance of their brain. This will only bring your child pain and turmoil. Their brain works the way that it is supposed to work. There is nothing that can change that.

WHAT THE DOCTORS CAN'T TELL YOU ABOUT LEVEL 3 AUTISM

Giving your child psychoactive drugs will only lead to seizures, dysregulation, meltdowns, and other unwanted side effects. Avoid the psychoactive drugs at all costs. You'll just have to take my word for it.

People with level 3 autism deserve their own separate category. There is no other condition in the world that is like level 3 autism. It needs its own diagnosis, separate from all the other mental, psychological, and cognitive conditions. Level 3 autism is a very specific condition that applies to a vey select group of individuals. It should not be lumped in with a bunch of other conditions that have absolutely nothing to do with it. When I explain what level 3 autism really is in the next chapter, everything that I am saying right now will become crystal clear. There are many mental and psychological conditions that may seem like level 3 autism, but it is in a league all its own. There is a fundamental difference between level 3 autism and these other conditions, which will be clear to you after reading chapter 2.

WHAT THE DOCTORS CAN'T TELL YOU ABOUT LEVEL 3 AUTISM

There is a part of me that believes that the term "autism" should no longer be used to describe people with level 3 autism. The word autism has become very generic. Everybody is using the term to describe themselves these days. Part of me thinks that a new word should be chosen to describe level 3 autism. But the truth is, if I'm being honest, is that the word "autistic" really resonates with me. It almost seems like the perfect word. I think that's why everyone wants to be autistic these days. It just sounds cool. I'll say this. If the word "autism" is ever replaced, it will have to be replaced with an even cooler word. I'm not sure if that is possible.

If I were to make my own "autism spectrum disorder" it would look completely different than the current model. I would also have 3 levels in my model. Level 3 would be people with profound autism. Level 2 would be people with "savant syndrome". Level 1 would be logical geniuses. Savant syndrome is the condition that comes closest to level 3 autism. A person with savant syndrome has a brain that works similarly to a person with level 3 autism. There are similarities but there are also key differences. A person with savant syndrome has a diminished amount of self-sufficiency. A person with level 3 autism has no self-sufficiency. The support needs are a little different between savant syndrome and level 3 autism as well.

The level 1 part of the spectrum refers to people who are very smart. The smartest people. People who are considered geniuses. People who have very high logical prowess. The people on the level 1 part of the spectrum would have certain autistic traits. I would consider myself on the level 1 part of the spectrum. I should point out that all true geniuses will suffer from emotional and psychological disorders. They will suffer from things such as depression, addiction, insomnia, and bad relationships. There is a difference between level 1 and levels 2 and 3. The difference is the support needs that each level on the spectrum requires. People at the level 2 and 3 parts of the spectrum cannot take care of themselves without help from other people. That is not the case for people on the level 1 part of the spectrum. They don't need help to take care of themselves. The extent of their support needs are therapists and psychiatrists. Because of this I can't consider the level 1 part of the spectrum to be true autism. I will talk more about geniuses in the next chapter.

The point that I am trying to drive home in this chapter is that it is time to take your level 3 autistic child off the spectrum. The spectrum does more to hurt your child than to help them. There is nothing that a doctor can do for you in terms of your child's level 3 autistic condition. They don't understand the condition. Level 3 autism is not a medical condition that can be treated. It is a difference in how the brain works. The time has come for me to explain exactly what level 3 autism is.

CHAPTER 2

THE TRUE DEFINITION OF LEVEL 3 AUTISM

Here is where things start getting good.

This is going to be the best part of the book for many of you.

This is the chapter where I explain exactly what level 3 autism is. This is the chapter where I explain exactly how level 3 autistic brains function. This is the chapter where I explain why your children behave the way that they do. This is the chapter where I explain exactly why your kids are so special.

In the brain there is a logical intelligence component and there is an emotional intelligence component. Your logical intelligence allows you to learn, comprehend, and memorize. Your emotional intelligence allows you to reason, rationalize, and empathize. In a typical brain, the brain devotes roughly equal resources to its logical intelligence component and its emotional intelligence component. The brain splits the resources between the logical intelligence component and the emotional intelligence component. This is how it works for a brain that doesn't have level 3 autism.

This is not how a brain with level 3 autism works. In a brain with level 3 autism, the brain doesn't devote any resources to its emotional intelligence component. It instead, devotes all its resources to the logical intelligence component. The resources that would normally be devoted to the emotional intelligence component of the brain are instead diverted to the logical intelligence component of the brain. What this means is that in a brain with level 3 autism, the emotional intelligence component of the brain doesn't work but the logical intelligence component of the brain has twice as many resources.

WHAT THE DOCTORS CAN'T TELL YOU ABOUT LEVEL 3 AUTISM

HOW THE BRAIN BALANCES INTELLIGENCE

Logical Intelligence a person's ability to:

1. Analyze

2. Memorize

3. Learn

Emotional Intelligence a person's ability to:

1. Reason

2. Rationalize

3. Empathize

WHAT THE DOCTORS CAN'T TELL YOU ABOUT LEVEL 3 AUTISM

This means that people with level 3 autism are purely logical people. They are the only purely logical people in the entire world. This is what separates them from everyone else. This is what makes them so unique. This is why I consider them miracles of creation. This is why their condition shouldn't be lumped in with other mental and psychological conditions. These people are truly in a class by themselves.

Your child, in reality, is a living, breathing supercomputer. For a person with level 3 autism, everything processes through the logical intelligence component of their brain. Their senses, their emotions, their speech, their awareness, all processes through the logical intelligence part of the brain. A person with level 3 autism lacks the ability to reason and rationalize. Instead, they rely exclusively on memorization.

WHAT THE DOCTORS CAN'T TELL YOU ABOUT LEVEL 3 AUTISM

NON AUTISTIC BRAIN

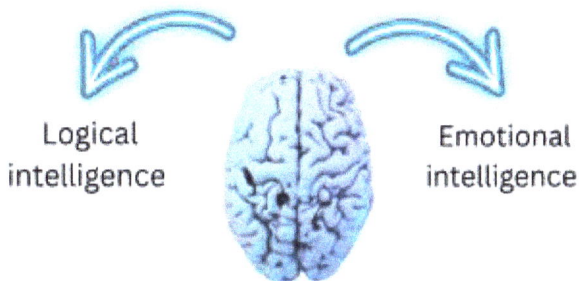

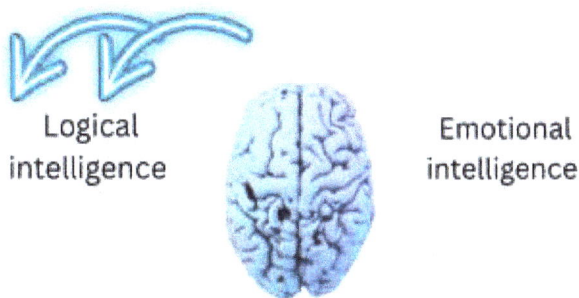

Logical intelligence

Emotional intelligence

AUTISTIC BRAIN

Logical intelligence

Emotional intelligence

WHAT THE DOCTORS CAN'T TELL YOU ABOUT LEVEL 3 AUTISM

All people with level 3 autism have extremely powerful memories. Far more powerful than people who don't have autism. Some people with level 3 autism have super-powerful memories. Speech and communication skills for someone with level 3 autism also relies on logic and memorization. This is why all people with level 3 autism are considered nonverbal. This doesn't mean that they can't say words or speak. It means that their ability to communicate with others is affected.

A person with level 3 autism doesn't have a way to communicate with you directly. They memorize what to say for specific situations. Logical frequencies are an exception to this. I will talk about logical frequencies in the next chapter. When you think of your child, you must think logically. You must think mathematically. You must think digitally.

I'm not going to downplay the disadvantages that come with level 3 autism. I'm going to be very clear. Because the emotional intelligence component of the brain does not work in someone with level 3 autism, they have no ability to reason or rationalize. They have no emotional awareness. This means that they will never be self-sufficient. They will have to be supported for their entire lives. There is nothing that will ever change this. Someone else will always have to be their emotional awareness for them. There is nothing that can change this. This is the reality of living with level 3 autism. The world that they perceive is different than the world that the rest of us perceive. When we think of intelligence, many of us think of logical intelligence. Many of us underestimate the importance of emotional intelligence and how it factors into everything that we do. People with level 3 autism should not be referred to as mentally disabled. The accurate term would be "emotionally disabled".

If a person with level 3 autism is considered emotionally disabled, then they should also be considered logically superior. They are logically superior to everyone and everything in this world. You read that correctly. There is no source of logical processing power in the world that compares to a level 3 autistic brain. There is

WHAT THE DOCTORS CAN'T TELL YOU ABOUT LEVEL 3 AUTISM

no other brain, computer, or machine in the world with the logical computation and processing power of a level 3 autistic brain. Some of you may be shaking your heads and rolling your eyes right now. I assure you that everything I just said is a fact. Everything I just said is the truth. Everything that I just said is reality. Your child has one of the most powerful logical brains on Earth. The only people who can compare are other people with level 3 autism. There is something else that I should mention. People with level 3 autism are better than everyone else at mathematics.

There is a catch. Because a person with level 3 autism lacks emotional awareness, they have no way to access their super-powerful brains. The only way they would be able to utilize their full potential is if someone else facilitated the situation for them. I have a feeling there aren't very many people who would be able to facilitate those situations. As a result, all we do is focus on the disadvantages of people with level 3 autism. We only focus on the things they can't do. Most people don't realize that they have any advantages, much less how to focus on them. Luckily for all of you, I am a person who can do that. The key to getting people with level 3 autism to realize their potential is through logical inputs and logical frequencies. I will talk more about that in the next chapter.

SAVANT SYNDROME

In the previous chapter I said that savant syndrome is the condition that is closest to level 3 autism. I will explain why I said that. I will explain how the brain of a person with savant syndrome works. In a person who has savant syndrome, the brain dedicates most of the resources to the logical intelligence component. It dedicates a small amount of resources to the emotional intelligence component. The brain dedicates 80-85% of its resources to the logical intelligence component and 15-20% of its resources to the emotional intelligence component. A person with savant syndrome is not purely logical. They are primarily or mainly logical. This means that they have a very powerful logical brain and a diminished amount of emotional intelligence. This means that they can be self-sufficient at a basic level. They will still need support, but not to the extent that someone with level 3 autism needs support.

The level 3 autistic brain has more logical processing power than a brain with savant syndrome. The savant brain has emotional intelligence and awareness, even though it is diminished. If people think that savants are geniuses, just imagine what a person with level 3 autism would be able to do if the proper situation were facilitated for them. A person with level 3 autism would be capable of far more impressive feats than a person with savant syndrome. If the proper situation is facilitated for them. A brain with level 3 autism is the most powerful source of logical processing in the world. A brain with savant syndrome is the second most powerful source. A person with savant syndrome has a small amount of access to their special abilities. A person with level 3 autism has no access to their special abilities unless someone creates the situation for them.

WHAT THE DOCTORS CAN'T TELL YOU ABOUT LEVEL 3 AUTISM

non autistic brain

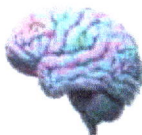

autistic brain

savant brain

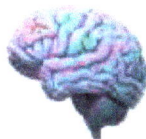

WHAT THE DOCTORS CAN'T TELL YOU ABOUT LEVEL 3 AUTISM

Some of you may be asking yourselves, why couldn't everyone just be savants?

I will give you my theory as to why some people are born with level 3 autism and others are born with savant syndrome. Keep in mind that my perspective is different from other people. I look at things from the perspective of nature and creation. This is my belief. I believe that if an autistic person needs to be born and there are no suitable parents/protectors. I believe that in this case Mother Nature will give the autistic child a small fraction of their emotional intelligence back to compensate for this. In nature I call this balance. This is just my theory. Do with it what you will.

This is the perfect time to talk about geniuses. The brain of a logical genius will normally be balanced 60-65% logical intelligence and 35-40% emotional intelligence. A logical genius has enough emotional intelligence to be self-sufficient. They don't need support to take care of themselves. However, their emotional intelligence is lower than average. This impacts their emotional and psychological well-being. People who are geniuses will suffer from depression, addiction, insomnia, and bad relationships as I mentioned in the previous chapter. When it comes to level 3 autism, savant syndrome, or logical geniuses, it all comes down to how the brain balances intelligence.

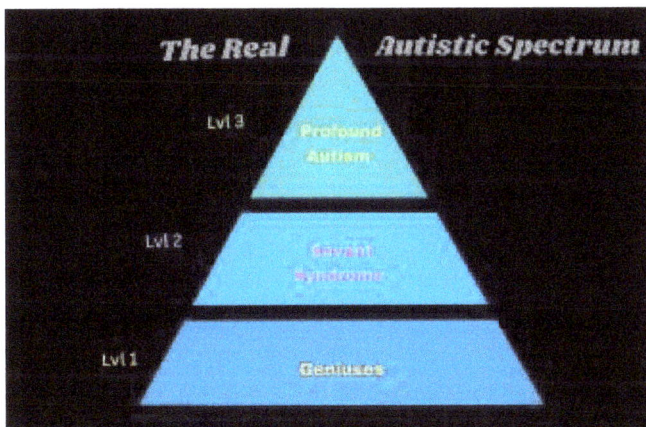

The Real Autistic Spectrum

Lvl 3 — Profound Autism

Lvl 2 — Savant Syndrome

Lvl 1 — Geniuses

To sum things up, the emotional intelligence portion of the brain is disabled in a person with level 3 autism. This means that they have no ability to reason or rationalize. They learn strictly through memorization. As a result of this the logical intelligence portion of the brain is overpowered. The brain devotes all its resources to the logical intelligence portion of the brain. This makes the level 3 autistic brain the most powerful source of logical processing in the world. It makes no sense to focus on the disadvantages of people with level 3 autism. We should instead focus on the massive advantages that they have.

FUN FACT ** People with level 3 don't have the ability to lie. They will always tell the truth. This doesn't mean that they can't get answers wrong. But they lack the ability to intentionally deceive someone.

I believe that many years ago in the past, people had a far more intelligent understanding of level 3 autism. I believe that in the past there was a far more profound (excuse the pun) understanding of level 3 autism than what exists in the world today. I believe that there was a time when people knew how to utilize people with level 3 autism to their full potential. This means that people with level 3 autism would have been very powerful tools in the hands of those who knew how to utilize them. I believe that many of the

WHAT THE DOCTORS CAN'T TELL YOU ABOUT LEVEL 3 AUTISM

legends that we have been told are based on people with level 3 autism. People with level 3 autism aren't just capable of amazing logical feats. They are also incredible strong. They don't have the emotional constraints and limiters that the rest of us have. They have access to 100% of their physical strength. To put that in perspective, the rest of us have about 60-70% access to our physical strength. If you have ever seen someone with level 3 autism have a meltdown, you will know what I am talking about. In that state, autistic people can be incredibly difficult to control or restrain. An autistic child having a meltdown may be too much for some parents to handle.

All that profound knowledge seems to have been lost somehow. Completely lost. No one in the world understands the condition of level 3 autism anymore. No one except for me. I have a very good understanding of the condition, but I doubt that I know as much as people did thousands of years ago. I do understand the condition well enough to know that many changes need to be made in order for my brothers and sisters to lead fuller lives.

I will end this chapter, leaving you something to ponder. I have explained in detail what level 3 autism is. I have explained that it is a condition where the brain disables the emotional intelligence component and devotes all its resources to the logical intelligence component. Is there a condition where the brain disables the logical intelligence portion of the brain and instead devotes all its resources to the emotional intelligence portion of the brain? What would this condition look like? How would this condition manifest itself inside of a person?

I am going to assume this condition doesn't exist. But if it does, I have just given doctors their reference point.

DOES THIS CONDITION EXIST IN THE WORLD?

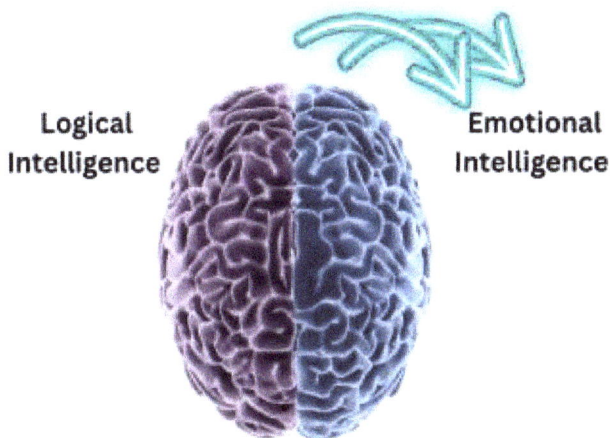

Logical Intelligence

Emotional Intelligence

CHAPTER 3

LOGICAL INPUTS AND LOGICAL FREQUENCIES

LOGICAL INPUTS

If you think about computers when you hear the term logical inputs, you are on the right track. In the same way that a computer uses logical inputs and outputs, this also applies to your child with level 3 autism. Your child's brain works in a purely logical fashion. This means that it functions very similar to how a computer would function. If you want good outcomes from your child, you must use good, logical inputs. This is the only way that you will get good, logical outputs.

I say logical inputs as opposed to emotional inputs. Let me explain. "Logical inputs" are concepts that your child's brain can process and understand. "Emotional inputs" are concepts that your child's brain can't process or understand. As I've stated before, your child's brain doesn't devote any resources to the emotional intelligence portion of the brain. It devotes all of the resources to the logical intelligence portion of the brain. This means that feelings and emotions process through the logical intelligence portion of the brain in your child. This means that it is far more difficult for your child to process emotion than logic. Logic comes second nature to your child. Emotion does not. This is very important to understand when you are trying to teach your child new skills. You must keep things as logically as possible and keep the emotion to a minimum.

LOGICAL INPUTS are superior.

EMOTIONAL INPUTS are inferior.

Emotional inputs at their best have low effectiveness. Emotional inputs at their worst are totally ineffective and may cause some regression. They can also cause confusion and instability. When it comes to your child learning, memorizing, or performing certain activities, logical inputs are a necessity. Good logical inputs will determine the level that your child is able to perform at. A person with level 3 autism learns exclusively through memorization. Because of this people with level 3 autism have very powerful memories. You will run out of things to teach them before they run out of space to store the lessons. People with level 3 autism will memorize what to say in certain situations and memorize what to do in other situations. Having a large amount of good logical inputs will increase your child's ability to conversate and perform certain activities. Emotional inputs will not help with any of this. As I said before, emotional inputs are ineffective for people with level 3 autism. Your children learn in a completely different way than people who don't have autism. Emotional inputs can be very effective for people who don't have autism. It is very important not to confuse these situations. The brain of a person with level 3 autism works differently. This means that different teaching methods will be needed for them.

Let me give you some examples of bad emotional inputs.

GOOD LOGICAL INPUTS

WHAT THE DOCTORS CAN'T TELL YOU ABOUT LEVEL 3 AUTISM

An example of a bad emotional input would be asking your child a "why" question. Your child has no way to understand, comprehend, or process "why" questions or statements. You will only confuse your child.

Another bad emotional input is asking your child "how they feel about something". Your child has no way to process or understand this question. You can ask your child how they feel, but you can't ask them how they feel about a particular situation. It will only lead to confusion.

The emotional intelligence part of your child's brain doesn't work. This means that they cannot process emotional or abstract statements and questions. How you phrase something can make all the difference. How you phrase a statement, or question will determine whether your child can accept an input. If you phrase the statement or question logically, there will be no problems.

Let me give you an example of phrasing something logically. Let's say I met a guy named Jack who happens to have level 3 autism. I want to introduce myself to Jack and then ask him if we can be friends. First, I will show you how I wouldn't phrase it:

"Hi Jack. My name is Dr. E. Can we be friends?"

"Hi Jack. My name is Dr. E. Can I be your friend?"

Now I will show you the way that I would say it:

"Hi Jack. My name is Dr. E. Can Dr. E and Jack be friends?"

"Hi Jack. My name is Dr. E. Can Jack be Dr. E's friend?"

Do you see the difference? In the second set of questions, I phrased them more logically. Saying or phrasing questions and statements in a logical way is what is beneficial for your child. Think of algebraic equations when you are speaking to your child. You can get your child to learn anything with the correct logical input. You can get your child to memorize anything with the correct logical input. You can teach your child to perform many more tasks with the correct logical inputs. Your child will function at a much higher level, in many different respects, with the correct logical inputs. It is much easier for your child to learn, understand, and process logic than it is for them to learn, understand, and process emotion. The latter is not even possible. Are you starting to see how important logical inputs are for your child? I will give you some more examples of bad emotional inputs. Then I will give you the correct logical inputs that you should be using.

BAD EMOTIONAL INPUTS:

"Why did you put your shoes on backwards?"

"What do you think about the Christmas lights?"

"The man fell down because he was clumsy."

"How does the food taste?"

ALTERNATIVE GOOD LOGICAL INPUTS

"You put your shoes on backwards."

"Do you like the Christmas lights?"

"The man was clumsy. The man fell down."

WHAT THE DOCTORS CAN'T TELL YOU ABOUT LEVEL 3 AUTISM

"Do you like the food?"

When you make abstract statements to your child or you ask them abstract questions, you will do nothing but confuse your child. You will also damage the progress that you are making with good logical inputs. Your child's brain works in a way that doesn't allow them to reason, rationalize, or ponder. When you ask your child to use the part of the brain that doesn't work, it causes conflicts for your child. These conflicts are bad for your child. They will damage your child's ability to perform. You must communicate with your child in a way that they can process and understand. You must be direct and to the point. When you communicate with your child in a way that they can process and understand, it makes it easy for them to give you appropriate responses. It gives them added stability. It allows them to perform at a higher level. I can't stress how important good logical inputs are for your child. I can't stress how bad emotional inputs are for your child. Good logical inputs are a necessity for your child.

WHAT THE DOCTORS CAN'T TELL YOU ABOUT LEVEL 3 AUTISM

Let me simplify all of this for you. It is far easier for your child to process logic than it is for them to process emotion. It is imperative that you understand this. You must always keep this in the back of your mind. You must talk to your child in a logical way. You must interact with your child in a logical way. You must do things in a logical way. This will make a ton of difference. If you do the things that I'm telling you to do, you will see changes. Remarkable changes. Your child will be able to do more things. Your child will be able to say more things. Their behavior will improve. This won't happen overnight. It will take patience and perseverance. But over time you will see improvements in your child.

What I'm telling you to do may go against some of your natural parenting instincts. This won't be easy for many of you. You will have to change. You must change. Not for your sake, but for the sake of your child. You must figure out ways to deal more logically with your child. This will require you to think outside of the box. You will have to learn to grow along with your child.

WHAT THE DOCTORS CAN'T TELL YOU ABOUT LEVEL 3 AUTISM

Another concern that I must address is that many parents see the things that other children can do and want the same things for their child with level 3 autism. This is a problem. This is a big problem. Emotional inputs can be very good and useful for someone who doesn't have autism. This is not the case with your child. Emotional inputs can be very bad and detrimental for someone with level 3 autism. You must understand and respect your child's condition. Your child perceives things differently. Your child understands things differently. Your child's brain works differently. There are certain concepts that your child will not be able to process or understand. What works for non-autistic children will not work for your child in most cases. There are many instances where you will not be able to do for your child what you seen parents doing for their non-autistic children. In many cases it's not about your child. It's about you. It's about what makes you feel good and not what is best for your child. By failing to accept reality you are setting your child up for overstimulation and dysregulation, and possibly meltdowns. When your child finally flips out, you are looking at them like they are the problem. Your child is not the problem. You are the problem. I will talk more about this in the next chapter.

All the logical inputs don't have to come directly from you. There are a wide variety of sources that can act as logical inputs. Computers can act as logical inputs. Flash cards can act as logical inputs. Puzzles can act as logical inputs. Legos can act as logical inputs. Board games can act as logical inputs. Video games can act as logical inputs. Musical instruments can act as logical inputs. Anything that you use logically can act as a logical input. You can teach your child to say or do anything with the correct logical input. The more logical inputs the better. There is no limit to how many good logical inputs you can give to your child.

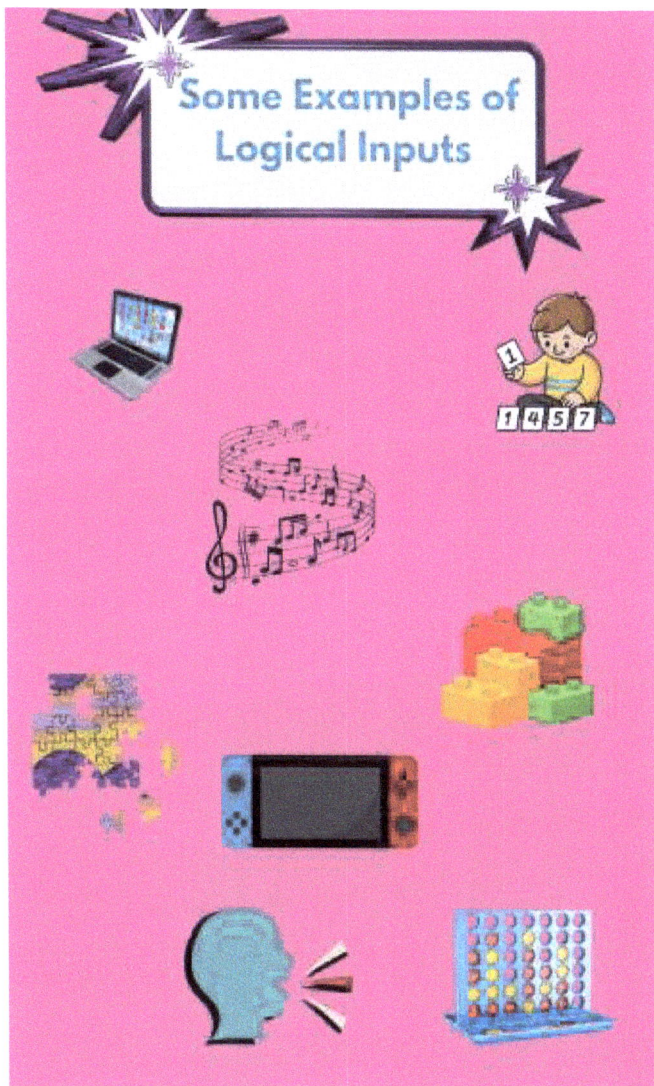

Some Examples of Logical Inputs

WHAT THE DOCTORS CAN'T TELL YOU ABOUT LEVEL 3 AUTISM

Your child doesn't learn through rationalization. Your child learns through memorization. There are many lessons that your child will not be able to process or understand. However, they can memorize those same lessons that they can't understand. As I said before, your child has a very powerful memory. There is no limit to your child's memory. The things that they can't learn, they can memorize. For example, you may not be able to teach your child how to use the bathroom, but you can have your child memorize how to go to the bathroom. You may not be able to teach your child how to cross the street, but you can have them memorize not to cross the street until they see the white light. What I'm trying to get through is that your child is far more capable than you imagine. It's all about teaching them in the proper way. Its's all about knowing how to utilize their powerful memories. It's all about using good logical inputs that your child can process and understand. If you do these things, your child will perform on a much higher level, and their behavior will be much more stable.

WHAT THE DOCTORS CAN'T TELL YOU ABOUT LEVEL 3 AUTISM

LOGICAL FREQUENCIES

Have you ever heard of people with level 3 autism having "special abilities" or "superpowers"? It's true. It's not a myth. To access those "special abilities" and "superpowers" you must understand logical frequencies. All people with level 3 autism have a frequency or frequencies that allow for supermassive or super powerful logical inputs. These supermassive and super powerful inputs will allow for supermassive and super powerful outputs. You can think of a logical frequency as a very powerful computer program. Logical frequencies give far greater access to a person with level 3 autism which allows for far more powerful inputs. Unfortunately, I am probably the only person in the world who understands the logical frequencies of a person with level 3 autism, and my knowledge is not that extensive. I know very little about logical frequencies in people with level 3 autism.

WHAT THE DOCTORS CAN'T TELL YOU ABOUT LEVEL 3 AUTISM

This is why I said this is a matter of science. I don't think doctors are equipped to handle logical inputs and logical frequencies. I think that scientists are better equipped to research and investigate logical inputs and logical frequencies. If scientists can crack the code of logical inputs and logical frequencies, they could then share this knowledge with the medical community. Doctors would then be able to formulate adequate medical plans for people with level 3 autism. They won't ever be able to cure level 3 autism. They could come up with medical plans to help with behavioral issues and plans to help people with level 3 autism function at a higher level.

I will now share the little knowledge that I do have about logical frequencies as they pertain to people with level 3 autism. I am aware of 3 logical frequencies. These 3 frequencies are:

Basic Logical Frequency – This frequency allows for anyone to use basic logical inputs on someone with level 3 autism.

Motherly Love Frequency – This is the communication frequency that is normally shared between a mother and her autistic child. The" motherly love" frequency allows for some emotional inputs to get through at times. It is not always available or reliable. It also allows for greater understanding of communication between a mother and autistic child. There may be things that the autistic child says that only the mother will understand. There may also be things that the autistic child will understand only if it comes from the mother. The "motherly love" frequency is not exclusive to mothers. Fathers, grandparents, siblings, teachers, etc. may also utilize the "motherly love" frequency.

Virtual Reality Frequency – I believe that there is a powerful logical frequency that exists within the virtual reality world. I believe that a person with level 3 autism will be able to do things in the virtual reality world that they can't do in the real world. I believe that a parent will have greater access to their child with level 3 autism in the virtual reality world than they will have in the real world. My entire research study in the last chapter is based on these concepts. These are just theories of mine, but I believe them to be true. The only way that I will now for sure is to conduct my research study. Let's all hope that I am able to make my research study a reality in the near future.

CHAPTER 4

DYSREGULATION AND MELTDOWNS

People with level 3 autism are at a disadvantage. But they have incredible advantages to compensate for this.

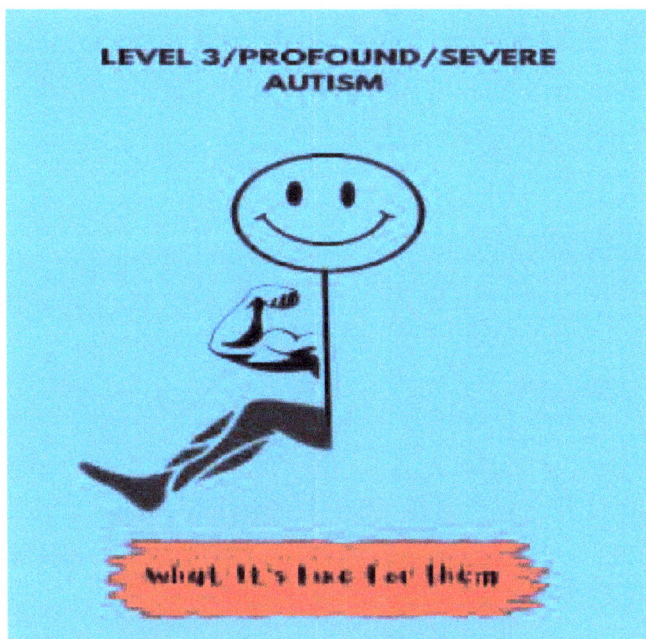

WHAT THE DOCTORS CAN'T TELL YOU ABOUT LEVEL 3 AUTISM

I am going to give you a different way to think of your autistic child. Think of your child as not having two arms and two legs. Think of them as only having one arm and one leg on one side of their body. The one arm and one leg that they have is incredibly strong and powerful.

The incredibly powerful arm and leg of the autistic person do them no good if they are not able to balance or stabilize the other side of their body. They will always need someone to support, balance, and stabilize the part of their body that doesn't have the arm and the leg.

If they are given the proper support, balance, and stability on the side of their body that doesn't work, they will be able to do amazing things with their incredibly powerful arm and leg.

I want you to think of level 3 autism exactly as I have just described it. A person with half of a working body will need support for their entire lives. They will always need someone to support the side of their body that doesn't work. There is nothing that will change this. The next thing that I want you to take from the illustration is how important balance and stability are for your child. If a person with one arm and one leg isn't given proper stability, they will function very poorly, if at all. Maintaining this stability is the full responsibility of the caretaker. It is your responsibility to make sure that your autistic child has a balanced and stable environment. Stable for them. Not for you. Another thing that I want you to take from the picture is how easy it is for your child to lose their balance and stability. How easy it is for them to become unstable. They rely 100% on you to maintain their balance and stability for them.

Now I want you to think about the illustration as it pertains to teaching your child. Is a person with one leg going to be able to walk the same way as a person with two legs? Can you teach a person with one leg to walk the same way as a person with two legs? No, you can't. You can't expect a person with level 3 autism to learn in the same way as people who do not have autism. The situations are totally different. The brains work differently. When you expect your child with level 3 autism to learn in the same way as a person without autism, you are basically tying their powerful arm behind their back. Or you are focusing your efforts on the side of the body without an arm and a leg. The focus should be on the side of the body with the powerful arm and leg. If a person with level 3 autism is given the proper support and stability on the side of their body that does work, they will be able to do incredible things with their powerful arm and leg.

Let's think about it from Mother Nature's perspective. Let's think about how Mother Nature incorporates balance. If a person doesn't have legs, their arms will become incredibly strong. If a person doesn't have arms, their feet will become very dexterous. If a person loses their sight, their hearing will become stronger. These are a few examples of how balance works in nature. This also applies to your child with level 3 autism.

We must follow nature's lead when it comes to dealing with people who have level 3 autism.

WHAT THE DOCTORS CAN'T TELL YOU
ABOUT LEVEL 3 AUTISM

The emotional intelligence half of the brain doesn't work. As a result, the logical intelligence half of the brain is twice as powerful. This gives a person with level 3 autism specific advantages and specific disadvantages. The time has come for us to start focusing on the powerful arm and leg, and not the side of the body that doesn't work. The time has come for us to focus on their powerful logical brains when we want to teach them and not the part of the brain that doesn't work.

I made the picture above to illustrate how important balance and stability are for your child. The picture shows you what balance and stabilization means for your child. If your child loses stability, they will become dysregulated. If your child becomes unbalanced, they will become dysregulated.

Many people may not be aware, but dysregulation can be a very serious situation for people who have level 3 autism. Especially when dysregulation leads to meltdowns. Meltdowns are no joke. They are not temper tantrums. Meltdowns can become very violent, dangerous outbursts. I explained that the emotional intelligence part of the brain doesn't work in people with level 3 autism. This means that they have no emotional limiters or constraints. This means that a person with level 3 autism has access to 100% of their physical strength. To put that in perspective, most people only have access to 60-70% of their physical strength. But it's not just that. Many times, our emotional intelligence will prevent us from doing bad things. Our ability to reason and rationalize may prevent us from doing something horrible. This doesn't apply to people with level 3 autism. There is nothing holding them back. When a person with level 3 autism is having a meltdown, you may find it extremely difficult to control or restrain them. A child having a meltdown may be too much for some parents to handle. When you are dealing with a person with level 3 autism having a meltdown, it may feel like you are dealing with a force of nature. When a person with level 3 autism is having a meltdown, they will probably not attack close family members. They will probably harm or injure themselves instead or damage property within the home. This may not be the case with strangers. If they are having a meltdown around people that they are not familiar with, they may attack them. This is something that you always must be aware of.

The first thing that I should explain is that people with level 3 autism have no control over dysregulation or meltdowns whatsoever. They don't ponder it. They don't plot it. They don't think about it. Dysregulation and meltdowns are a physiological or reflexive reaction to stress or anxiety within their environment. Dysregulation and meltdowns are not the fault or responsibility of people with level 3 autism. It is the fault of the caretaker. It is your fault and your responsibility. Whether its parents, grandparents, or teachers, whoever is taking care of the person with level 3 autism is responsible for controlling their environment. Dysregulation and meltdowns always come from something that is negatively impacting your child in the environment. I've created a picture detailing the main causes that can lead to dysregulation and meltdowns. I am going to talk about each one in detail:

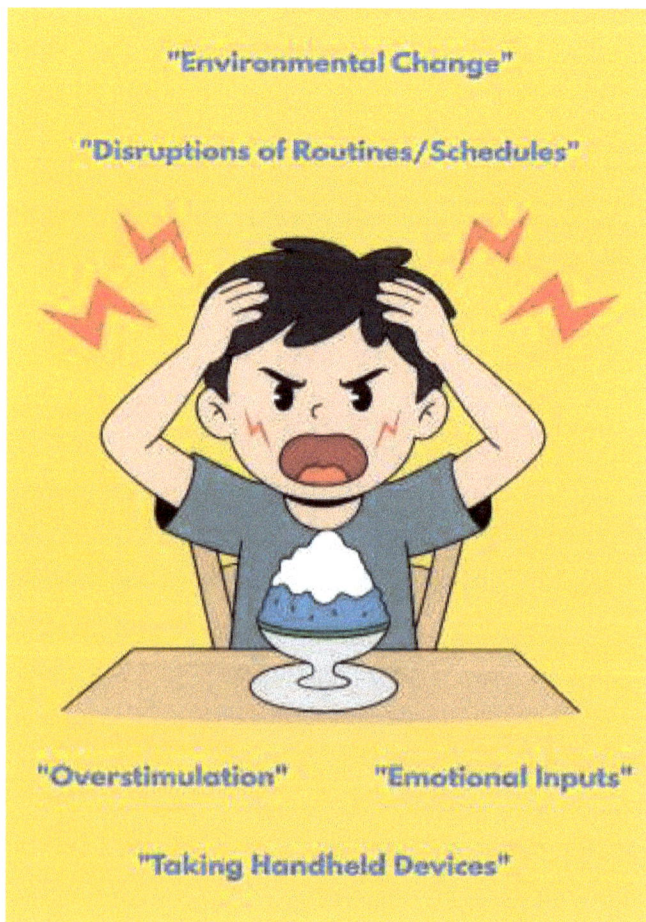

WHAT THE DOCTORS CAN'T TELL YOU ABOUT LEVEL 3 AUTISM

ENVIRONMENTAL CHANGE

Environmental changes affect all people with level 3 autism to some extent. But it affects some more than others. Environmental changes can affect some people with level 3 autism in a very negative way. It can lead to dysregulation and even meltdowns in some autistic people. Environmental changes can affect people with level 3 autism in different ways. Some people may only notice changes in their room. Others may notice changes in the house. There are some who will notice changes wherever they go such as schools, churches, libraries, restaurants, etc. You may have guessed that "change" is not the friend of your autistic child. People with level 3 autism don't like change.

Here is a trick you can try at home. Have your child draw a picture or write something on a piece of paper. They can even do arts and crafts if that is better. Have your child then place their creation somewhere in the room. Make sure that no one ever moves the creation from where they have placed it. If they always see their creation where they left it, the other changes made in the room may not bother them as much. Just a trick you can try.

DISRUPTIONS TO ROUTINES AND SCHEDULES

Disruptions to routines and schedules can lead to dysregulation and meltdowns very quickly. I've dedicated an entire chapter to routines and schedules in this book, so I don't want to talk a lot about it here. Routines and schedules serve as anchors. Routines and schedules give your child stability. People with level 3 autism rely on these routines and schedules. When you disrupt them, you are disrupting their stability. This is why disrupting routines and schedules lead to dysregulation and meltdowns so quickly. If you must disrupt your autistic child 's routines and schedules, you had better have a suitable replacement ready. Or a suitable alternative. I will talk more about this in the next chapter.

OVERSTIMULATION/SENSORY OVERLOAD

Overstimulation is at the core of most dysregulation and meltdowns. I explained earlier in the book that a person with level 3 autism processes their senses and emotions through the logical intelligence part of their brain. They don't have emotional intelligence to balance their senses and emotions. What they see. What they hear. What they smell. What they taste. What they touch or, touches them. All these things can lead to overstimulation. Overstimulation can lead to dysregulation, which can lead to meltdowns. All people with level 3 autism are highly susceptible to overstimulation or sensory overload.

Their emotions can also lead to overstimulation. Fear, anxiety, and frustration can all lead to overstimulation. Even joy and happiness can lead to overstimulation. A lot of parents will be fooled by this. A lot of parents will see their child smiling and happy and then begin to overstimulate them by doing what is making them happy too much. Too much happiness can also lead to dysregulation. If your child seems overly happy, you must be careful. I should really focus on this. This situation can fool many parents. Most parents want to see their children happy. They like to see their children smile. The more that they see their children smile, the better that they feel. This is not the case with people who have level 3 autism. This can be a bad thing. A very bad thing. Too much joy and happiness are no different than too much anxiety and stress. Any emotion that causes your child to become unbalanced or unstable will lead to overstimulation. Which will lead to dysregulation. Which will lead to meltdowns. This includes joy and happiness. If your child is smiling for too long, they are on their way to becoming overstimulated and dysregulated and possibly having a meltdown. You will wonder why your child is happy one moment and then flipping out the next moment. You will think that there is something wrong with your child. There is nothing wrong with your child. The problem is with you and your lack of understanding. If you see any emotion in your child's face for too long, it will lead to problems. Your child is at their most balanced and stable when their face is expressionless. Your child is not an emotional person. They are logical people. If their face doesn't show any emotion, they are in a good place. If you see any emotions on their face for too long, including smiling, overstimulation is on its way. This will be hard for many parents to grasp. People with level 3 autism have the most beautiful smiles. You want to see those beautiful smiles. This is a case where you must think about what is best for your child and not what is best for you. An emotionless face is what is best for your child. Many of you want to see your child happy. Happiness is not what is most important for your child. Balance and stability are what is most important for your child.

This will be hard for many parents of children with level 3 autism to grasp. Most of the time your child will not want to be bothered. They will want to be left alone. They don't want to be touched. They don't want to be talked to. They want to be left alone to engage in some sort of logical activity. This won't always be the case. There are times when they will want to be touched. There are times when they will want to be talked to. When a person with level 3 autism rubs their face against yours, this is their way of saying "I love you". However, these times are far less frequent than you would imagine.

Your child doesn't want to be bothered most of the time. They aren't looking for affection. They aren't looking for socialization. The key is to have adequate logical activities for them to engage in. Give them a logical activity to do and then let them do it. Let me reiterate. Your child doesn't want to be talked to all the time, and they don't want to be touched all the time. This leads to overstimulation and dysregulation. Learn how to keep your child engaged with logical activities, and then just leave them alone. People with level 3 autism are very susceptible to overstimulation. Overstimulation can lead to many bad situations. Routines and schedules are also very helpful regarding logical activities.

WHAT THE DOCTORS CAN'T TELL YOU ABOUT LEVEL 3 AUTISM

Dysregulation is the point where your child is either going to stim or have a meltdown. Dysregulation is normally preceded by overstimulation, but that is not always the case. There are times when your child will bypass overstimulation and go right into dysregulation. When this happens the window for calming them down and getting them back to a balanced, stable state becomes much smaller. When this happens, a meltdown is normally imminent. Some things that can lead to instant dysregulation are doom-scrolling on an electronic device or disrupting routines and schedules. These are things that can bring meltdowns very quickly. There are others as well.

If you are lucky, your child may engage in stimming as opposed to having a meltdown. Let's have a conversation about stimming.

STIMMING

Stimming is the way that a person with level 3 autism regulates their behavior. If they are stimming, they are regulating themselves. This is their self-defense mechanism to prevent dysregulation and meltdowns. Stimming is a good thing. It is better than the alternative of dysregulation and meltdowns. Stimming all the time however is not necessarily a good thing. If your child stims constantly this means that they must regulate their behavior constantly. That shouldn't be the case. If they constantly have to stim, then something in the environment is negatively impacting them. They don't stim on purpose. They don't become overstimulated on purpose. They don't become dysregulated on purpose. They don't have meltdowns on purpose. They have no control over any of these behaviors. These behaviors are a physiological reaction to something that is negatively impacting them in their environment. You can also think of these behaviors as reflexive. If your child is exhibiting these behaviors, then you need to go stand in front of a mirror. You then need to point your finger at the person that you see in the mirror. You are in total control over your child's environment. It is your responsibility to make sure that their environment is balanced and stabilized. They have no way to do it on their own. So, whenever your child is overstimulated, dysregulated, or having meltdowns, it is your responsibility. It is your fault. Your child doesn't have the ability to reason or rationalize. They don't have the ability to plan or plot. When something negatively impacts them in their environment, they are going to react physically.

The reason why so many kids with level 3 autism find themselves overstimulated and dysregulated is because of their parents and caretakers. They put their autistic children in situations that will overstimulate them. It's not really the parents' fault. They think they are doing good things for their children. They want to do the same things for their child that they see other parents doing for their children. They want to raise their children in the same way that they see other parents raising their children. That is the problem. And it is a big problem. Your child is not the same as other children. Their brain works differently. The things that work for kids who don't have autism will negatively impact your child. If we want to be fair to people with level

WHAT THE DOCTORS CAN'T TELL YOU
ABOUT LEVEL 3 AUTISM

3 autism, then we must respect their level 3 autistic condition. But before we can respect their level 3 autistic condition, we must understand their level 3 autistic condition. That is the problem. Most parents don't have a true grasp of their child's condition. They don't really understand. Hopefully this book will change that.

Your child is not looking to build friendships. They are not looking to be socialized. They don't like big parties. They don't like a lot of excitement. They don't like loud music. They don't like being around a lot of people. They don't like change. Some probably don't like to be touched very often. They are not interested in the same things that children without autism would be interested in. They don't want to be the life of the party. They just want a calm, peaceful, balanced, stable, logical environment. That is what is good for your child with level 3 autism.

While we are talking about overstimulation I should mention "food". Let's talk about what you feed your child. If you have found a couple of healthy options that your child likes to eat, just stick with those healthy options. Variety is not your friend. You shouldn't experiment with your child's food choices. As I explained earlier, people with level 3 autism don't like change. This includes what they eat. Eating is more complicated for people with level 3 autism than it is for other people. Every time they eat something, they must consider the taste, the smell, and the texture. Texture is how it feels on their tongue. Your child may not be able to eat certain foods depending on the way that they taste, smell, or feel. Don't force them to eat foods that they don't like. Find a couple of healthy options that they like and just stick with those. If they ask for the same thing every day, just give it to them. As long as it's healthy.

EMOTIONAL INPUTS

Emotional inputs can be defined as anything that your child can't understand or mentally process. I talked about two of the big emotional inputs in the last chapter. Asking "why" questions and making "why" statements is one of the worst emotional inputs. Your child has no way to understand or process "why". Asking your child how they feel about something is also another bad emotional input. The way that your child's brain works doesn't allow them to understand or process abstract statements or questions. These abstract statements and questions will confuse your child. Which can lead to anxiety. Which can lead to dysregulation. Which can lead to meltdowns. Emotional inputs are like a foreign language to your child. They have no way to understand them. If your child takes in a lot of emotional inputs at once, I can guarantee that your child will become dysregulated and probably have a meltdown. I'm going to give you a few scenarios in which your child may be exposed to a lot of emotional inputs at once:

Taking your child to the movies

If you take your child to see a movie, you must know that they won't be able to understand most of the movie. If you take them to see a children's movie, they may be able to follow the characters, and colors, and songs. I would be very careful about which movies you take your children to see.

Letting your child watch tv programs and videos

This is like watching movies. When your child watches television programs and videos, there will be a lot that they won't be able to process or understand. This is also taking in a lot of emotional inputs at once. This can lead to dysregulation and meltdowns. You even have to be careful with the kid's tv shows and videos. There could be a lot in those tv shows and videos that can overstimulate your child.

Doom scrolling on cellphones and laptops

Doom scrolling on a phone or laptop can also expose your child to a lot of emotional inputs at once. I once had a conversation with a parent whose child had a meltdown in the medical office. She had given her phone to her child, and he began to doom scroll. Very shortly after that, he was having a meltdown. I will talk about this parent and her child later in the book. By doom scrolling on the cellphone, her child was exposed to too many emotional inputs at once. Information that his brain could not process.

Emotional inputs will also degrade the progress that you make with logical inputs. You must learn to avoid using emotional inputs as much as possible.

TAKING THEIR HANDHELD DEVICES

This is a big one. I am sure that many parents of children with level 3 autism have experienced some sort of turmoil dealing with their children and handheld devices. They have probably had to deal with overstimulation and dysregulation. They have also probably experienced turmoil when trying to take away the handheld devices from their children. Think about how you would feel if someone took your cellphone from you. Think about how you would feel if you lost your cellphone. That feeling is magnified in your child. Handheld devices serve as an anchor for your child. They give them an added sense of stability. When you take away your child's handheld device, you are taking away one of their anchors. You are taking away a piece of their stability. One thing that you should have learned from this chapter so far, is that when you negatively impact your child's stability, there is going to be a problem.

If you do give your child a handheld device, you must control 100% of the access that they have to the content on the device. You can't just give them the device and let them do whatever they want to. You must make sure that they have no access to doom scrolling. You also must make sure that they don't have access to apps or games that will cause them overstimulation or dysregulation. If you decide not to give your child a handheld device, I would give them something that they can always keep with them. It could be a picture, a keychain, a squeeze ball, etc. Something that can serve as an anchor for them. It will give them extra stability.

WHAT THE DOCTORS CAN'T TELL YOU ABOUT LEVEL 3 AUTISM

Now if a parent or caretaker takes away the handheld device of child with level 3 autism, it can cause a problem. If someone outside of the home takes away your child's handheld device. Someone that they don't see in a position of authority. It can lead to an even bigger problem. Some of you may not grasp the seriousness of this situation. I will tell you the story of Brendan Depa to put this into perspective for you.

Brendan Depa was a 17-year-old mentally challenged young man living in Florida. I was unable to find Brendan Depa's exact medical diagnosis, but he was described as autistic. I don't think he had level 3 autism. If we go by the autistic spectrum, I assume that he would be considered level 2. It was clear from listening to him speak that he was mentally or psychologically impaired in some way. He had stayed in several group homes because of his disabilities. I should probably also mention that he was large and black.

When Brendan Depa was 17 years old, he was sitting in the hallway at his school, playing with his Nintendo Switch. A teacher's aide came up to him, took away his Nintendo Switch, and then walked away. Brendan Depa got up, followed behind her, and knocked her to the ground. He then proceeded to beat her senseless. Several people had to pull Brendan Depa off the teacher's aide. If they hadn't intervened, things may not have turned out well for the teacher's aide. The police came to the school and arrested Brendan Depa.

WHAT THE DOCTORS CAN'T TELL YOU ABOUT LEVEL 3 AUTISM

When I first read this story, the first thing that came to mind was a level 3 meltdown. I don't think that Brendan Depa has level 3 autism. I don't think. Apparently, people with level 3 autism aren't the only people who are susceptible to meltdowns. I don't know what Brendan Depa's exact medical diagnosis is, but I am certain that he is mentally and/or psychologically impaired in some way. His reaction wasn't a normal reaction. Brendan Depa's reaction was the reaction of someone who is mentally or psychologically impaired. That was a meltdown. He snapped. He probably had no idea what he was doing when he was doing it. So, what happened to Brendan Depa? What was his fate?

Brendan Depa was tried as an adult. His mental and/or psychological impairments were not taken into consideration. I want to talk for a moment about why this attack happened. Was Branden Depa sitting in the hallway waiting to attack someone? Did he single out the teacher's aide because he was bored?

WHAT THE DOCTORS CAN'T TELL YOU ABOUT LEVEL 3 AUTISM

Brendan Depa attacked the teacher's aide because she took his handheld device. She took his Nintendo Switch and walked away with it. He was clearly provoked. I'm not downplaying the teacher's aide's injuries. I'm sorry that this happened to her. But she clearly brought this on herself. Let me ask you all a question. How many of you would go up to a big, black guy, who is clearly mentally impaired, and take his possessions away, and just walk away with them? Does that seem like an intelligent thing to do? I wouldn't do it. I'm a badass and I still wouldn't do it.

During Brendan Depa's trial, the teacher's aide took no responsibility for her role in the incident. She testified for the prosecution. She wanted Brendan Depa to get jail time. The prosecutor also felt that Brendan Depa should receive jail time. The prosecution felt that a mentally impaired teenager should receive jail time. Brendan Depa was sentenced to 5 years in jail and 15 years' probation. A mentally impaired teenager who was clearly provoked was sentenced to 5 years in jail and 15 years' probation. In my opinion, this court ruling was not only cruel and unusual, but it was sick and disgusting. I don't know if it was because of incompetence. I don't know if it was because of racism. Brendan Depa was clearly railroaded. I'm not the only one who has condemned this decision. The Autism Society of America also put out a press release condemning the court ruling.

I told you this story for a reason. If your child has a meltdown and hurts or injuries someone, they could find themselves in legal jeopardy. You can't take for granted that the court systems will be competent or fair to your child. The Brendan Depa case should teach you that. You must be vigilant in ensuring that your child never ends up in a situation like Brendan Depa.

What I want you to take from this chapter is that your child needs you to support them. Your child needs you to keep them balanced. Your child needs you to keep them stable. They need you to control their environment and everything within their environment. They rely on you 100% for this. They have no control over this themselves. When your child becomes overstimulated. When you child becomes dysregulated. When your child has meltdowns. It is your fault. Not theirs. They have no control over their physiological reactions when they are negatively impacted by the environment. It is your responsibility to control their environment for them.

CHAPTER 5

ROUTINES AND SCHEDULES

In the previous chapter I talked about anchors. I also talked about balance and stability. Routines and schedules are anchors for your child. Anchors that give your child an added sense of balance and stability. I have explained that your child has a very powerful logical brain. The most powerful logical processing brains in the world. There is no logic that your child doesn't have the ability to understand and process. Provided they are given the proper logical inputs. And provided that bad emotional inputs aren't degrading the logical inputs. Routines and schedules are logical. Routines and schedules are things that your child can easily grasp and process.

WHAT THE DOCTORS CAN'T TELL YOU ABOUT LEVEL 3 AUTISM

Your child can understand and process anything that is logical. This includes numbers, dates, days, times, weeks, months, and years. If they are given the proper logical inputs, these concepts are child's play to someone with level 3 autism. You may not realize this, but your child has a photographic memory. Your child also has a very powerful sense of time. Far more powerful than you can imagine. As you create the routine, the more detailed information you give your child pertaining to the date and the time, the better. This is a good way to teach your child new concepts. This is a good way to teach your child about the various aspects of time. Time is mathematical. Mathematics is logical.

When you schedule an activity for them, make sure that they are aware of the month, the year, the date, the day, and the time. The more detailed and stringent the schedules and routines are the better. As I said before, they will give your child an extra layer of balance and support. It gives them support when they can rely on doing specific activities daily at certain times.

Routines and Schedules

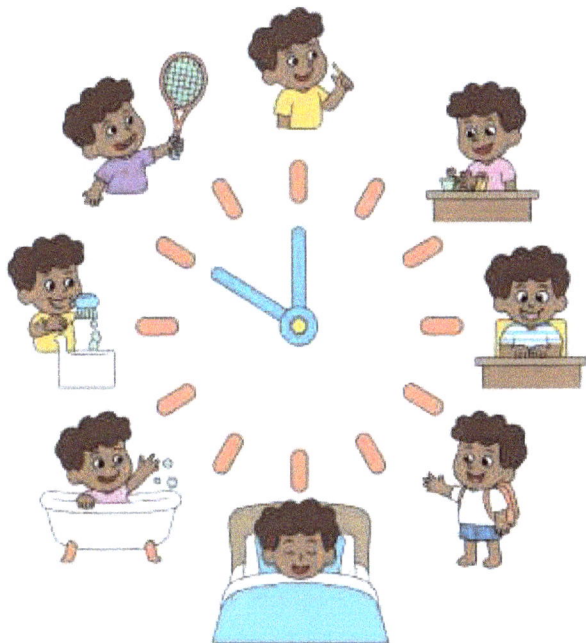

Are Very Important!!!

WHAT THE DOCTORS CAN'T TELL YOU ABOUT LEVEL 3 AUTISM

You can use routines and schedules to your advantage. I believe that computers, laptops, video games, and handheld devices are good for your child. They are logical, digital devices that are a natural fit for your child. If they are utilized responsibly. You must always be aware of overstimulation. You must completely control the access that your child will have to programs and games. You must be aware of this 100% of the time. Once you have the content under control, you can schedule your child's access to these devices on the routine. It will make using the devices more stable for your child when they are aware of the time, they can start using them and the time that they must stop using them. You can do this for all their electronic devices. This may not happen all overnight. It may take some patience and some vigilance to get them used to the routine. But once they are used to the routine, they will never forget it.

There is a catch to all of this. Once you have established a routine for your child, you must never disrupt it. Disrupting your child's routines and schedules can lead to a big problem. A very big problem. Disrupting your child's routine or schedule can lead to immediate dysregulation and meltdowns. When you come up with the routine, you must make sure that it is a routine that you can maintain. If you can't maintain the routine, it will lead to big problems. If you must change your child's routine or schedule you had better have a suitable alternative or replacement ready. You must then explain to your child in a logical way what the substitution is that is taking place. Just explain what the substitution is. Don't explain why the substitution is taking place. Always avoid "why" questions and statements with your child. These are emotional inputs that will confuse your child.

I cannot overstress the importance of routines and schedules for your child. It is a huge part of their support, balance, and stability. The more complex the routine is, the better it is for your child. Just don't make it more complex than you can handle. There is another advantage to routines and schedules. Once you have your child engaged in a logical activity that is scheduled, you can use that time for yourself.

WHAT THE DOCTORS CAN'T TELL YOU ABOUT LEVEL 3 AUTISM

You may use that time to take a shower. You may use that time to do some cleaning. You may even use that time to rest and relax. The point is that routines and schedules are powerful tools for both your child and you. You can use routines and schedules to have a very powerful effect in your child's life.

CHAPTER 6

SOCIAL MEDIA SUPERSTARS WITH LEVEL 3 AUTISM

In this chapter I am going to talk about two exceptional young men that I follow on Facebook. Both young men have level 3 autism. I will explain in great detail how differently level 3 autism impacts both young men. The names of the two young men are Cody and Darius.

"CODY SPEAKS"

WHAT THE DOCTORS CAN'T TELL YOU ABOUT LEVEL 3 AUTISM

"DARIUSKINGOFSTIMMING"

"IRISA NICKIE LEVERETTE"

I follow Darius and Cody on Facebook, so I have included their Facebook channels. They could also be on YouTube, Tik Tok, and Instagram.

Darius and Cody are two exceptional young men. They would both be considered prodigies in the level 3 autistic world. I don't have the words to express how much I like and admire these two individuals. I have watched a lot of their videos. Cody and Darius both have level 3 autism, but they are two very different individuals. The way that level 3 autism looks for Cody is not the way that it looks for Darius. There are similarities between Darius and Cody. But there are also a lot of differences. I will attempt to tell the stories of these young men from what I have gained from watching their videos. I plan for this to be educational and entertaining.

Let's start with the parents. From the videos it looks like Darius' mom is a single mom. I don't know if his father is around, but it appears that his mom handles most of the responsibilities. Cody has a mom and dad who work together. These three parents are some of the most amazing people in the world. I will deliver some harsh criticism later in the chapter, but don't let that fool you. I truly love and admire all three parents. They are truly amazing and inspirational. There is no doubt in my mind that these parents love their children with every fiber of their being.

WHAT THE DOCTORS CAN'T TELL YOU ABOUT LEVEL 3 AUTISM

Both Darius and Cody live in beautiful homes. They both have everything that a kid could ask for. They both have swimming pools. They both have trampolines and swings. They both live near parks. They are always very well dressed. They both are very well taken care of by their parents. I am giving you my perspective from the many videos that I have watched.

I have explained before that you can't compare a child with level 3 autism to a child who doesn't have autism. The situations are completely different. There are also times when you can't compare two people who have level 3 autism. Darius and Cody both have level 3 autism, but it affects them in completely different ways. Their situations are completely different. They are both prodigies and I am happy to share their story from my perspective.

Darius seems to be very food driven. Darius likes to eat. In a lot of Darius' videos, you will hear him say "go to the park". Darius appears to enjoy going to the park. You will often see Darius carrying a guitar in his videos. Darius is a good swimmer and likes to swim. I've recently seen Darius playing the harmonica and he was pretty good. I've also seen videos where Darius' mom is teaching him how to cook. Darius' mother says he is in the 15th grade, meaning he has been going to school for 15 years. That is astonishing. I have a feeling that there aren't many kids with level 3 autism who have gone to school continuously for 15 years. When you watch Darius' videos you will notice that he stims a lot. Darius stims quite frequently in the videos. His stimming is normally musical and melodious. Sometimes Darius' speech is not very clear.

Cody seems to be driven by videos. Cody's mother lets him perform certain tasks that allow him to earn dollars. Cody uses those dollars to order videos online. Cody seems to know and like a lot of the kid's characters such as SpongeBob and Thomas the Train. Cody has a very powerful photographic memory. Cody remembers everything no matter where it is. He remembers exactly how things are arranged wherever he goes. Cody also speaks very clearly.

WHAT THE DOCTORS CAN'T TELL YOU ABOUT LEVEL 3 AUTISM

Cody can also say no to something that he doesn't like. Cody uses a computer a lot. I don't think Cody likes to swim. Cody does like to swing. In Cody's videos you will often see his mom have Cody get rid of trash and unused possessions to earn dollars. Cody speaks so well that there are times when you may not realize that he is non-verbal. Cody functions at a very high level. If you were to compare Cody to other people who have level 3 autism, he would stand out as exceptional. Cody can do things that a lot of people with level 3 autism wouldn't be able to do. This comes at a cost. Cody is very susceptible to overstimulation, dysregulation, and meltdowns. This is not unusual. In the non-autistic world, people with strong logical prowess often suffer from depression, addiction, insomnia, and bad relationships. It appears that most people with high logical prowess will have a cross to bear whether they have autism or not.

I would say that Cody functions at a much higher level than Darius. Darius, however, has a huge advantage over Cody. I mentioned that Darius stims a lot. Darius uses his stimming to regulate his emotions and behavior. Darius can stim his way through most overstimulation and dysregulation. Darius is almost bullet-proof when it comes to overstimulation, dysregulation, and meltdowns. This allows Darius to do a lot of things that Cody won't be able to do. This is why Darius has been able to go to school continuously for 15 years.

I want to talk about two very memorable videos I have seen from both Darius and Cody.

There is a video where it's Cody's mother's birthday. Cody is singing happy birthday to his mother. And it sounds amazing. I couldn't believe it when I was watching the video. I would bet a million dollars that you can't find another person with level 3 autism who can sing happy birthday to their mother in the way that Cody did. Cody is truly special. This is a good time to bring up his father. Cody's father is a master at talking to him logically. I am impressed with this man every time I hear him speak to Cody. He should teach classes for other parents to learn how to speak logically to their autistic kids.

Darius also has a video that I found very memorable. There was a time that Darius was stimming. It was musical. Darius' mother started tapping her foot to Darius stimming. It actually sounds very good. Darius grabbed his mother's leg and stopped her from tapping her foot. I thought this was so funny. Now I should mention that Darius' mother shouldn't be joining in on Darius' stimming. That is a mistake. That is why Darius grabbed her leg and stopped her. I would bet a million dollars that you will never find a person with level 3 autism who has the regulatory control over their emotions and behavior that Darious does. Darius is also truly special.

I want to talk about some very important and good things that Cody's mother and Darius' mother have done. Darius knows how to swim. This is very important because one of the leading causes of death in people with level 3 autism is drowning. So, it's very important that Darius knows how to swim. I applaud Darius' mother for ensuring that he knows how to swim. I encourage all of you to make sure that your children know how to swim. I also want to talk about something very important that Cody's mother is doing. She is reaching out to other parents who have children with level 3 autism. This is very important. We need to form a level 3 autism community. A community that is self-enclosed. A community that doesn't acknowledge any other mental or psychological condition. A community that reaches out to and supports each other. A community that shares with each other. What Cody's mother is doing is an important first step in forming these communities.

Now I'm going to talk about something that won't be very pleasant. I'm going to talk about the mistakes that I see the parents making in their videos. These mistakes are very egregious. They are very bad. Mistakes that are having massive negative impacts on Darius and Cody. I will be harsh at times. I'm not going to sugarcoat what I see in these videos. Just know that I am not

WHAT THE DOCTORS CAN'T TELL YOU ABOUT LEVEL 3 AUTISM

picking on these parents. They were wonderful enough to share their experiences with us. All of you are guilty of the same mistakes that these parents make. Some of you make even worse mistakes. The reason is because none of you truly understand the condition of level 3 autism. And there is another reason that I will talk about a little later. Let's get started.

I'm going to start with Darius' mother. She does a lot of really good things. She has Darius on a routine. She doesn't use a lot of logical inputs that I hear in the videos. But the mistakes that she makes are really bad. I feel that she has no real understanding of what overstimulation is. Let's start with the breakfast ritual that she has with Darius. This breakfast ritual disgusts me every time that I see it. She gives Darius this huge plate of food. When Darius tries to eat his food, she asks him questions. She pulls his plate away from him. She then starts singing this ridiculous song "chill on the plate". Darius can't even make it through his breakfast without stimming. I saw Darius wearing a "chill on the plate" t-shirt so I'm guessing his mother is very proud of this ridiculous ritual. It is unbelievable the crap that she puts Darius through when he simply wants to eat his breakfast. You really need to see it for yourselves. It is a very good lesson in everything that you shouldn't do with your autistic child. I wouldn't even do this nonsense with a child who doesn't have autism. Can you imagine what Darius is going through when all he is trying to do is eat breakfast. It's worse for him than for people without autism. This has nothing to do with not understanding the condition. This ritual is just disgusting. I don't know what benefit she thinks Darius is getting from this. If she was worried about him choking, she could easily cut the food up into smaller portions or give him one portion at a time. Instead, she gives him this huge portion of food just so she can sing the stupid "chill on the plate" song. I really think that she thinks that the stupid song will make her famous. I hope that she reads this, because that ridiculous breakfast ritual needs to stop immediately.

The ridiculous breakfast ritual isn't her only mistake. I've seen videos where she plays loud music and dances all around Darius. Excitement is not a good thing for your children. Excitement leads to overstimulation and dysregulation. Balance and stability are what your child needs. A boring life is very good for someone with level 3 autism. Now I will talk about the video that has made me more upset than any of her videos. There is a video where she says that Darius has gotten off the bus with a lot of energy. She then makes him stand on a vibrating plate. Darius clearly doesn't like the plate. She forces him to stand on the plate. This is the first video where I saw Darius show anxiety in his face. Normally Darius doesn't show a lot of emotion and when he does, he is normally happy. This was the first time I saw him show anxiety. This was totally unnecessary. She could have had him jump on a trampoline. She could have let him go swimming. She could have let him swing on the swing. I found this video quite sickening, and I actually shed a tear. Darius' mother gets away with things that other parents of autistic children will never get away with. Darius has the most powerful regulatory control that I have ever seen.

WHAT THE DOCTORS CAN'T TELL YOU ABOUT LEVEL 3 AUTISM

He can stim his way almost out of any situation. She would not get away with any of this stuff with someone like Cody.

Another mistake that Darius' mother makes is that she tries to participate when Darius is stimming. I can't begin to explain how inappropriate this behavior is. It is an invasion. When your child is stimming, they are regulating themselves. This is not the time to join in with them. Stimming is very private and personal to the person with level 3 autism. Trying to join in is interference. It is very bad. It is very childish. And as I stated before it is very inappropriate. I hope that all of you reading this never engages in that behavior.

WHAT THE DOCTORS CAN'T TELL YOU ABOUT LEVEL 3 AUTISM

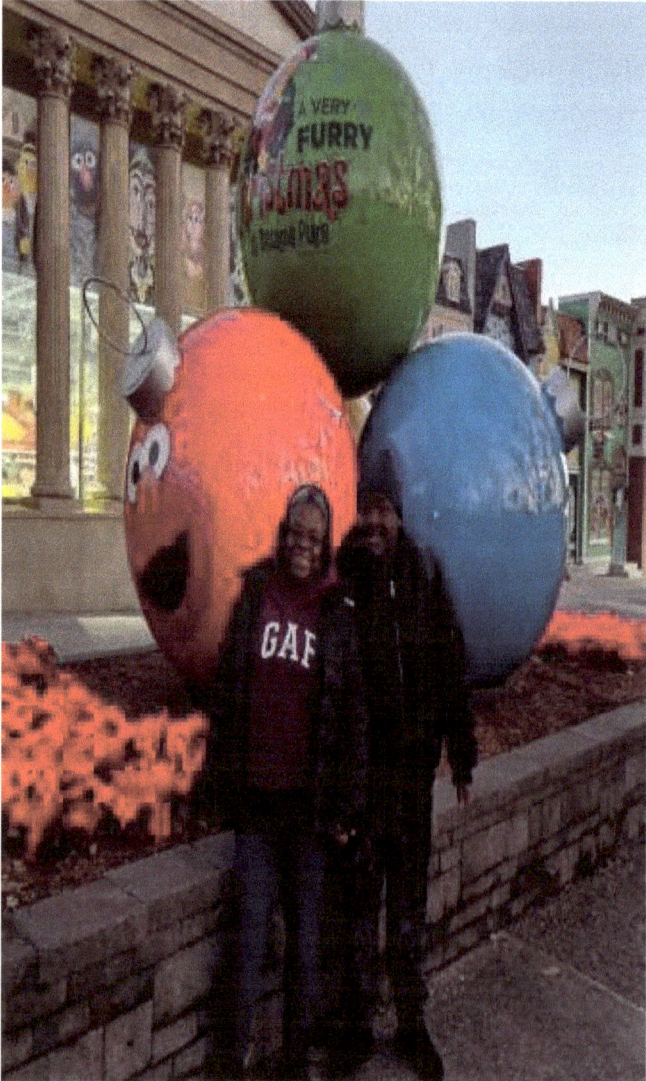

WHAT THE DOCTORS CAN'T TELL YOU ABOUT LEVEL 3 AUTISM

Because Darius is stimming for most of the day, his brain doesn't have many resources left for learning and performing activities. Darius has been in school for 15 years and has a professor for a mother, but you can barely understand what he is saying. His speech is not very clear. There are a lot of things that Darius can't do. Darius should be performing at a much higher level. The problem is that instead of learning, Darius is constantly regulating. The reason for this is his mother. She overstimulates him all the time. I'm not even sure if she can help herself. Because she is a professor, I think she feels that she can teach Darius in the way that she teaches her other students. She will never be able to do this. It is simply not possible. Darius' brain works completely differently. This applies to all people with level 3 autism. My advice to Darius' mother would be to calm down and chill out. Stop being so hyperactive. Give Darius a stable and balanced environment. Give Darius some peace. Especially at breakfast time. If she listens to my advice Darius will perform at a much higher level than he is currently performing at.

WHAT THE DOCTORS CAN'T TELL YOU ABOUT LEVEL 3 AUTISM

Now I will talk about the mistakes I see happening in Cody's home. These mistakes are very bad too. The mistakes that I see in Cody's home have a highly negative impact on Cody. Let me get the father out of the way first. I've only seen him make one mistake in the videos. There are times when Cody's mother is talking to him and the father joins in at the same time. This results in a situation where both parents are talking to Cody at the same time. This is a no-no. Only one parent should be talking to Cody at a time. He should be allowed to focus on one parent at a time. Now on to the mother, who makes the worst mistakes. She uses a lot of emotional inputs. She uses a lot of abstract statements and questions. Statements and questions that Cody has no way to process or understand. This confuses Cody many times. She's also experimented with several medications on Cody. Cody appears to be more dysregulated then ever since taking the medicine. I just heard his mother say they are considering putting a helmet on Cody to keep him from biting himself. The medicine has done him no good.

WHAT THE DOCTORS CAN'T TELL YOU ABOUT LEVEL 3 AUTISM

Think about this. How can a doctor prescribe medicine for a condition that they don't understand. They can't. It makes no sense. There is no medicine that will change your child's condition. There is no medical procedure that will change your child's condition. They only thing you will accomplish by giving your child medicine for their autism is seizures, dysregulation, meltdowns, and a bunch of other nasty side effects.

The mother also seems insistent in socializing Cody. I have heard Cody say "no friends" in many of his videos. This tells me that Cody doesn't like to be around people. His mother is not getting the message. I forgot to mention it, but Darius' mother is also guilty of this. Both parents seem to be intent on forcing their children to be socialized. When you force your autistic children to be around people who are different from them, you are forcing your child to become a spectacle. Your child is very limited in their ability to interact with other people. Forcing your children into these situations will cause them anxiety and overstimulation. Socialization may benefit you the parent, but it rarely benefits your child.

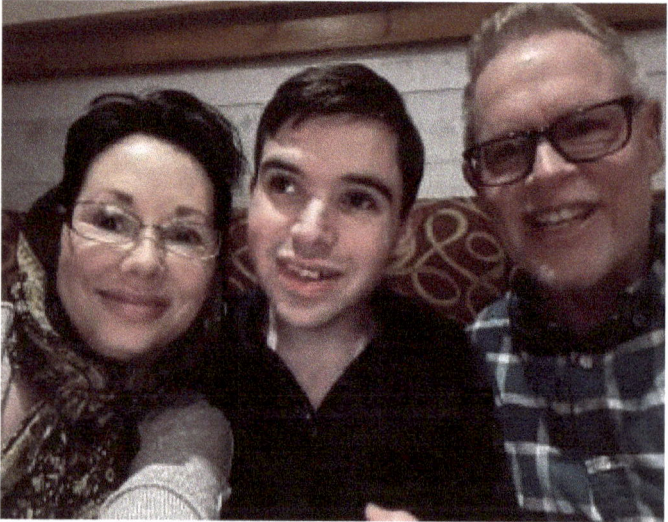

The problem with Cody's mother is that she has another son named Justin. Justin doesn't have autism and is completely self-sufficient. She wants the same life for Cody that Justin has. That is never going to happen. It is not even a possibility. Cody will need care and support for his entire life and Justin will not. Justin can take care of himself and Cody cannot. There is nothing that is going to change this. I don't think that Cody's mother can accept this reality. She always says that she is not trying to cure autism, but that is exactly what she is trying to do. And Cody is paying the price for this. She uses a lot of emotional inputs. She tries to medicate Cody's autism. She puts Cody in a lot of bad situations that overstimulate him. She is the person causing his dysregulation. The worst part of all of this is that she thinks that this is all Cody's fault. She thinks that something is wrong with Cody. Not only can she not accept reality, but she also can't seem to accept responsibility. This isn't Cody's fault. This is her fault. If Cody is becoming dysregulated, then something in the environment is dysregulating him. It's not his responsibility to control his environment. He has no way to control his environment. He is totally reliant on someone controlling and maintaining his environment for him. I have seen videos where Cody's mother is telling him that he is losing things because he had a meltdown. It's like she's punishing him for having meltdowns. Cody has no way to process that. It's totally ridiculous.

WHAT THE DOCTORS CAN'T TELL YOU ABOUT LEVEL 3 AUTISM

Let me speak about this helmet situation. I think that Cody is 25 years old. He is at least that old. Now his mother wants to make him wear a helmet, so he won't keep biting himself. The biting has gotten bad lately. I wonder why that is. I'm going to make a prediction. I predict that forcing Cody to wear a helmet will bring along a whole new set of problems. I predict that Cody's mother is making another bad decision. I'm going to make another prediction. If things don't change in Cody's home, Cody will eventually end up in a facility or an institution. I know that Cody's fans don't want to see that. I don't want to see that. I know that Cody's mother means well. I know that she is trying to do her best for Cody. I know that she has good intentions. But the road to Hell is paved with good intentions. That is what is happening here with Cody. Cody's mother must accept reality. She can't raise Cody in the way that she raised Justin. She has to be a completely different mother for Cody than she was for Justin. Cody will not have the same opportunities that Justin has. Cody is not going to own his own home. Cody is not going to get married and have children. Cody will need to be supported for his entire life. There is nothing that can change this. If she can't accept that reality, Cody will continue to be the one who suffers.

This doesn't just apply to Cody and Darius. This applies to all people with level 3 autism. If something in the environment is causing them overstimulation and dysregulation, it is your responsibility to find it and fix it. If your child is having meltdowns, then take a good look in the mirror. It is never your child's fault. It is always your fault. Many of you want to raise your children in the way that parents raise their children who don't have autism. The situations are completely different. Your child's brain works differently. Your child thinks differently. Your child perceives things differently. Your child sees the world in a completely different way. A lot of the things that are good for children without autism will be detrimental for your children who do have level 3 autism. You must understand and respect the level 3 autistic condition. I have said the same things many times throughout the book. I really want certain points to stick with you.

This is the advice that I would give to Cody's mother. I would put Cody on a stringent routine filled with logical activities. Activities that Cody can process and understand. Activities that are not going to overstimulate Cody. This will give Cody an added sense of balance and stability. The more that Cody is busy with logical activities, the less chance that there will be for overstimulation and dysregulation. Stop the friends. Stop socialization. Stop the parties. Stop the medication. Stop the emotional inputs or abstract statements. If she takes my advice, Cody's self-injurious behaviors will decrease significantly. One thing that I didn't mention before is that Cody also kicks holes in the wall when he has meltdowns. I believe that this behavior would also decrease significantly if my advice is listened to.

There is one good thing about Cody's mother that I forgot to mention. She has the most wonderful tone. She speaks in a very calm and soothing manner. She always speaks this way to Cody. I am positive that the frequency of her voice resonates very well with Cody.

There is one more thing that I should mention about Cody's mother. I've spoken to her before on a chat. It was only once. And it was brief. I explained to her why her son had a meltdown at the Dr.'s office. I then explained to her my vision for an assisted living facility geared exclusively towards people with level 3 autism. I explained my vision in great detail. That was the only time I ever talked to her. She does know how to reach me. I really hope that she contacts me again in the future. I would be more than happy to help her and her husband as it pertains to Cody. This goes for all of you reading this book. I will help anyone in any way that I can if they are taking care of somebody with level 3 autism.

There are some things that all of you need to understand. You can't bully your child into self-sufficiency. You can't punish your child into self-sufficiency. You can't medicate your child into self-sufficiency. Your child will never be self-sufficient. They will need care and support for their entire lives. There is nothing that will change that. There is no one who can change that. That is a reality that all of you must accept. If you are unable to accept that reality, your child is the one who will suffer. Worse than that, when reality finally catches up to you, you will not be prepared. I may have sounded harsh in my criticisms of these parents. The truth is that I have the utmost admiration and respect for these parents. I know that they are doing the best that they can. I have no doubt that they love their kids more than anything else in the world. They make critical mistakes because they don't understand the level 3 autistic condition. That is one reason. There is another reason that these parents make mistakes. The same reason that all of you will make the same mistakes. The reason is fear. The same fear that all parents of children with level 3 autism are going to have. The fear of what happens to your child when you are no longer able to care for them and support them. I understand that fear and I have an answer. I have a solution.

WHAT THE DOCTORS CAN'T TELL YOU ABOUT LEVEL 3 AUTISM

The solution is assisted living centers that cater only and specifically to people with level 3 autism. Assisted living centers that have employees who are trained to understand what the level 3 autistic condition really is. Assisted living centers that have employees who are trained to give your child the care and support that they will require when you are no longer able to. If you know that there are facilities that can care for and support your child when you are no longer able to, it will remove a huge burden from your shoulders.

There is one very important key to these assisted living centers. One very important key to ensure their effectiveness. The key is employees who fully understand what the level 3 autism really is. These facilities will need to hire employees who understand how to dispel dysregulation. They will need employees who are constantly on the lookout for overstimulation. They will need employees who know how to bring your child out of a meltdown. They will need employees who know how to interact logically with your child. They will need employees who understand how your child's brain works. They will need employees who understand the importance of balance and stability. They will need to understand the harm that emotional inputs can cause. They will need to understand the complexities of eating for people with level 3 autism. They will need to understand that your child's primary way of learning is through memorization. They will need to understand the advantages and disadvantages of level 3 autism. They will need to understand the importance of routines and schedules. They will need to know that medicine will never be a cure for the level 3 autism condition. They will need employees who understand all these things and more. These assisted living facilities will not only need employees who fully understand what level 3 autism is, but they will need to hire employees who are sympathetic towards the condition. They will need to hire people who want to help your children. This is the only way that these assisted living facilities will be effective.

How do we make this solution a reality. I don't have the answer to that question. Not yet. It will take a collaborative effort from all of us in the level 3 autism community. We all will have to step up to make this solution a reality. If you have a child with level 3 autism, I encourage you to make videos. Share your experiences with the rest of us. We can all learn from each other's experiences. I have learned a lot from watching Cody's and Darius' videos. I encourage all of you to watch their videos. You can learn a lot about what to do and not to do.

CHAPTER 7

FINAL THOUGHTS

First things first.

Many of you are wondering how I can be so knowledgeable about level 3/profound/severe autism. Many of you are wondering if you should believe me. Many of you are wondering if you should trust me. I can't make that decision for you. My suggestion would be that you should take me seriously. I happen to know what I am talking about.

I didn't go to school to learn about level 3 autism. I haven't studied level 3 autism for years. If I had done those things, it wouldn't have made any difference. I wouldn't know any more about level 3 autism than any of you. I was given my knowledge and understanding of level 3 autism from a very high source. It would be very hard to explain my source, so I won't even attempt to explain it. I was given this knowledge and understanding for a very simple reason. To improve the quality of life and make the world a better place for your children.

I'm going to assume that Mother Nature was sick of her miracles being mistreated and marginalized. I'm also going to assume that Mother Nature thought that it was time for this to change. So, Mother Nature called on the big guns. She enlisted the services of the Modern Day Prophet. I was given this knowledge and understanding because I am the most qualified to use it. There is no one better qualified to help people understand the true nature of your child's condition. I consider all of your children to be my logical brothers and sisters. You can think of me as Mother Nature's ambassador appointed to work on behalf of your children.

I am the only Metaphysical Infinitarian in the world. My perspective of the Creator and creation is based on my understanding of 0's and 1's. This means that my perspective of the Creator and creation is purely logical. Your children are purely logical people. My connection to your children is through pure logic. I have a purely logical connection with your children. This is why I consider them my logical brothers and sisters. My entire focus and purpose in life is to improve the quality of life and to make the world a better place for my logical brothers and sisters. The first step in that process is making sure that everyone understands what level 3 autism really is. That is the purpose of this book. I have explained many things about level 3 autism in this book that I'm sure that parents were not aware of. A lot of this may not make any sense to you but as I said earlier in the chapter, I am the "real deal". You all have a new BFF. You all have someone who is on your side. Someone who happens to know what they are talking about.

The first thing that I explained is that your child needs to come off the autistic spectrum. The spectrum does not benefit your child. All it does is confuse the understanding of your child's condition. Your child's condition is unique and there are no other mental or psychological conditions that are like it. The support needs of your child are completely different than these other conditions. Savant syndrome comes close, but the support needs are still different. Level 3 autism is in a class of its own and it deserves 100 % scrutiny and analysis. The focus needs to be entirely on level 3 autism alone and no other condition. It's not that I don't have sympathy for these other conditions, but they get plenty of support. The people with level 3 autism are the ones not getting adequate and proper support.

I want it to be clear that my problem is not with doctors. The problem is that doctors don't fully understand what level 3 autism is. Once they have a better understanding of the condition, then hopefully we will be able to better rely on doctors for care and support for people with level 3 autism.

Do not give your child medication in an attempt to treat their autism. It will not work. Even if the doctors did understand the condition, which they don't, they would never be able to prescribe medication to treat level 3 autism. It would be the same as prescribing a child without autism medication to give them level 3 autism. That is not possible. The reverse is not possible either. The only thing that you will accomplish by giving your child medication is seizures, dysregulation, meltdowns, and a bunch of nasty side effects. There is no medication, no medical or surgical procedure that will change how your child's brain works.

I explained to you how the brain works for someone with level 3 autism. For a person with level 3 autism, the brain doesn't devote any resources to the emotional intelligence part of the brain. It devotes all the resources to the logical intelligence part of the brain. The emotional intelligence part of the brain doesn't function in a person with level 3 autism. This means that your child doesn't have the ability to reason or rationalize. This means that your child will need to be supported for the entirety of their lives. There are certain concepts that they have no way to process or understand.

It's not all bad, however. People with level 3 autism have certain advantages over people who

WHAT THE DOCTORS CAN'T TELL YOU ABOUT LEVEL 3 AUTISM

don't have autism. People with level 3 autism learn exclusively through memorization. This means that people with level 3 autism have very powerful memories. Far more powerful than the memory of a person without autism. People with level 3 autism are also the most powerful logical processors in the world. To put this simply, they are better at math than everyone else. We need to stop focusing on the disadvantages of people with level 3 autism and start focusing on their advantages.

You must communicate with your child in a way that they can process and understand. Any concept that they can't process or understand I refer to as an emotional input. Any concept that they can process and understand, I refer to as a logical input. You should only use logical inputs with your children. You can teach your child pretty much anything with the correct logical inputs. Logical frequencies allow for powerful inputs. I'm only aware of two logical frequencies currently. The "motherly love" frequency and the "virtual reality" frequency. We will have to rely on the scientists to help us figure out the other logical frequencies.

You should do your best to avoid using emotional inputs. Emotional inputs will cause confusion and lead to anxiety and dysregulation. Dysregulation can lead to meltdowns. Meltdowns can turn into very bad situations very quickly. When your child is having a meltdown, they will become very strong and difficult to control. If they were to hurt someone during a meltdown, it could lead to a very bad legal situation.

Let me be very clear about something. When your child is overstimulated. When your child is dysregulated. When your child is having a meltdown, it is not their fault. It is never their fault. It is your fault. It is always your fault. You are responsible for controlling your child's environment. If something in their environment is causing them overstimulation, dysregulation, or meltdowns, it is your responsibility to find out what it is and fix it. Part of the problem is that many of you want to raise your children the way that you see other children being raised. This is a problem. Your child is different. You must understand and respect that. What is good for children who don't have autism will be detrimental for children who do have autism. You put your children in situations that aren't good for them and then you are dumbfounded as to why they are overstimulated and dysregulated.

Excitement and parties are not good for people with level 3 autism. Joy and happiness are not critical. Balance and stability are critical. There is nothing more important than balance and stability for someone with level 3 autism. There are many things that can cause your child to become overstimulated. What they see, what they hear, what they smell, what they taste, what they touch, and what touches them can all lead to overstimulation. Overstimulation can lead to dysregulation and meltdowns. Any emotion that lingers too long in your child can lead to overstimulation. This includes joy and happiness. Your child is always in their best place when they aren't showing too much emotion. The less emotion they show, the better off they are. Stimming is a good thing. It is a way for your child to regulate their behavior and emotions. They shouldn't be stimming all the time, however.

Make sure that your child has daily scheduled routines. When your child knows that they have daily activities to look forward to at a specific time each day, it will give them an extra sense of balance and stability. Routines can be very helpful to you. Just make sure that you manage the routines. If your child is expecting to do something and it doesn't happen, it will lead to some serious problems such as dysregulation and meltdowns.

I talked about two gentlemen with level 3 autism that I like and admire very much. Their names were Darius and Cody. I follow them both on social media. I encourage you to do the same. I have learned a great deal from watching these videos. I dedicated this book to these two exceptional young men. I encourage all of you with children who have level 3 autism to make videos and share your experiences. The more people that we have sharing their experiences, the more that we will learn. It will increase the depth of our understanding.

I may have sounded harsh in my critique of the parents that I talked about. It was not my intent to sound mean or to hurt anyone's feelings. These parents aren't the only ones making mistakes. All of you are. Some of you are making worse mistakes. I can't sugarcoat these mistakes. They are too harmful to my brothers and sisters. My first priority is the well-being of people with level 3 autism, and that includes Darius and Cody. The feelings of parents come secondary. The reason that all of you are making these mistakes is because you don't understand what the condition of level 3 autism really is. The parents don't understand the condition. The doctors don't understand the condition. The ABA therapists don't understand the condition. Luckily, I do understand the condition. I have made it my mission to make sure that the entire world understands the condition.

WHAT THE DOCTORS CAN'T TELL YOU ABOUT LEVEL 3 AUTISM

WHAT THE DOCTORS CAN'T TELL YOU ABOUT LEVEL 3 AUTISM

Your child doesn't want to be touched or felt all the time. Don't let other people touch or feel your child. Your child doesn't want to be talked to constantly. Your child wants peace. They want quiet. They want balance. They want stability. Don't pester your child and don't let other people pester your child. You should always keep an eye on your child. Learn how to keep an eye on them from a distance. Your child is very sensitive to overstimulation, whether it comes from you, somebody else, or some other source. I want to make a suggestion. I suggest letting your child be the one to initiate affection. When your child gets close to you and touches your face, and rub their face against yours, that is their way of saying "I love you". Let them be the ones to say it first. Let me make another suggestion. Instead of letting your kids watch Spongebob and Bugs Bunny, let them watch instructional and educational videos. Let them watch videos teaching them mathematics. Let them watch videos teaching them words and sounds. Let them watch videos teaching them how to use the bathroom. Let them watch videos teaching them how to cross the street. Let them watch videos teaching them how to swim. Let them watch videos teaching them how to play musical instruments. You get the point. Let them watch videos that help them advance but won't overstimulate them. As I've said many times throughout this book, we have to focus on your child's advantages and not their disadvantages. You have to keep things logical for your child. There is no amount of logic that your child can't absorb. There is no logic that your child can't process. Keep your child busy with logical activities. Keep your child on a routine and schedule. You will be surprised at the level your child will start to perform at. This will also cause dysregulation and stimming to subside. This won't happen overnight. This will take patience and perseverance. If you stay vigilant with what I said, you will see results.

We have to come together as a community. We have to close ranks. We must put the focus squarely on level 3 autism. We can't allow any other conditions to be considered. We have to reach out to each other. We have to communicate with each other. We have to support each other. We have to help each other. We don't have anybody else. All we have is each other. It is time that we started acting like it. We need to create a very powerful level 3 autism community. One that has to be taken seriously. One whose voice can't be drowned out.

Let's talk about the biggest fear and concern that all parents of children with level 3 autism have. That fear is what happens to their children when they are no longer able to care for or support them. Who will take care of your children when you are no longer able to? I have an answer to that question.

The answer is assisted living centers that focus exclusively on level 3 autism. Assisted living centers with employees who are trained to care for and give your children the support that they require. That is the answer. That is the solution. We will all have to come together to make that solution a reality.

How many of you feel bad that you have a child who has level 3 autism? How many of you wish

WHAT THE DOCTORS CAN'T TELL YOU ABOUT LEVEL 3 AUTISM

that you had a child who was born non-autistic? Let me give you a different perspective. What if instead of your child being born with level 3 autism, they turned out to be evil? What if your child turned out to be a murderer? What if your child turned out to be a rapist? What if your child turned out to be a gang member? What if your child turned out to be a drug dealer? What if your child turned out to be a monster? What if instead of dealing with level 3 autism, you were dealing with expensive court costs and lengthy prison sentences? What if autism saved your child?

People with level 3 autism can't be evil. They can't be monsters. Like so many of the rest of us. The part of the brain that causes those situations doesn't work in your child. Being born non-autistic does not guarantee that a child will have a good life. There are things in the world that are far worse than autism. Something to think about.

I have created a research study that explains how virtual reality can have a positive impact on people with level 3 autism and their parents. The research study is in the back of the book. I invite you all to look at it. I think you will find it very interesting. Speaking of virtual reality, there is something else that I would like to mention. I would like to see app developers like Meta, Microsoft, and Sony start developing games and applications with people who have level 3 autism in mind. I would like to see them focus on games and apps that can entertain and teach people with level 3 autism without overstimulating them. Games and apps that are designed to take advantage of your child's superior logical capabilities. I would also like to see employment opportunities created for people with level 3 autism. As I have said throughout the book, people who have level 3 autism are capable of things that the rest of us are not. Once their talents are better understood, I would like to see their talents monetized.

I have explained many things in this book concerning level 3 autism. I have explained many things that none of you have ever seen before. I have explained many things that you were not familiar with. I have explained many things that you may not be able to process on the first read-through. Some of you will need to read this book multiple times to fully grasp the things that I have said.

I have explained exactly what the condition of level 3 autism is. I have explained exactly how the brain works in someone who has level 3 autism. I have explained numerous times the advantages and disadvantages that come along with this condition. I have explained why it is far easier for your child to process logic that it is for them to process emotion. I have explained why logical inputs are so important when it comes to your child being able to learn and perform. I have explained how emotional inputs can degrade progress. I've explained why people with level 3 autism are so susceptible to overstimulation. I have explained how overstimulation can lead to dysregulation and meltdowns. I have explained why balance and stability are the most important things for someone with level 3 autism. I have explained how helpful routines and schedules can be for your children. I warned you to keep your child away from psychoactive medications. There is no medicine or medical procedure that can treat level 3autism. There never will be. Level 3 autism is not a medical condition. It is a difference in how the brain works.

I explained how we need to create a strong community that only focuses on people who have level 3 autism. It is imperative that people understand and respect this condition. I have even explained what can be done for your children when you are no longer able to care for or support them. My end goal is to make the world a better place for all people with level 3 autism. This means I want the world to be more accommodating to the condition then it currently is. This will only come with understanding and respecting the condition as I have said so many times throughout this book. I want everyone reading this book to help me accomplish my goal. If you all help me, I promise that I will be your child's biggest and most powerful advocate.

There is one last thing that I forgot to mention. You should all watch the movie "Rain

WHAT THE DOCTORS CAN'T TELL YOU ABOUT LEVEL 3 AUTISM

Man" if you have never seen it before. If you have seen it before, watch it again. It is an excellent movie. It does a tremendous job of explaining what life is like for a middle-aged man with level 3 autism. Dustin Hoffman won an award for his role in the movie. If you are taking care of someone with level 3 autism you must watch this movie.

WHAT THE DOCTORS CAN'T TELL YOU ABOUT LEVEL 3 AUTISM

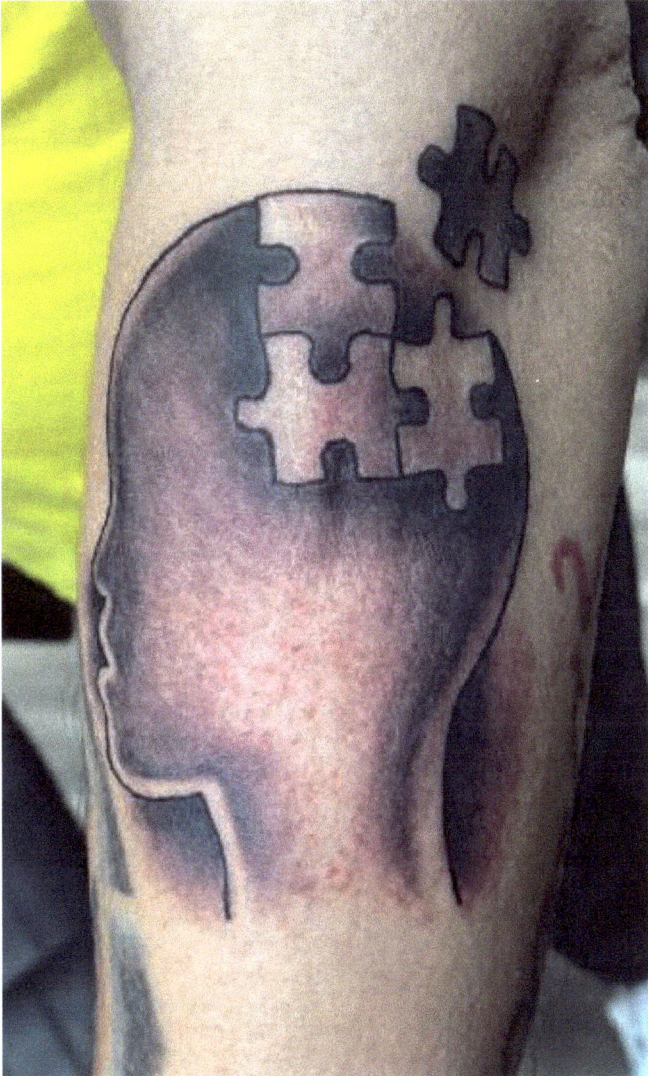

CHAPTER 8

VR-LEVEL 3 AUTISM RESEARCH STUDY

VR LEVEL – 3 RESEARCH STUDY

The purpose of this research study is to prove the positive impact that Virtual Reality can have on people with level 3 autism.

ABOUT ME

My name is Erskine Gibson. I also refer to myself as the Modern Day Prophet. Let's just say that I know and understand things that would be impossible for other people to understand. One of the things that I have a profound (no pun intended) understanding of is Level 3 Autism. I understand level 3 autism from the perspective of Mother Nature. This means that I understand level 3 autism in a way that differs from doctors and parents. It would be accurate to say that there is no one in the world who understands level 3 autism in the way that I do. This is why no one else has ever proposed this type of study. No one else can. No one else understands the logical inputs and outputs of someone with level 3 autism. No one else understands the logical frequencies. I am the only person in the world who can successfully perform and carry out this research study.

LEVEL 3 AUTISM

You may or may not be familiar with level 3/profound/severe autism. I am not going to give you the medical definition of Level 3 autism. I am going to explain level 3 autism from my perspective and the perspective of Mother Nature. Which will prove why I am the most appropriate person to conduct this research study.

In most brains, the resources are balanced between your emotional intelligence and your logical intelligence. In a brain with level 3 autism there are no resources dedicated to the emotional intelligence component of the brain.

WHAT THE DOCTORS CAN'T TELL YOU ABOUT LEVEL 3 AUTISM

In a brain with level 3 autism all the brain's resources are dedicated to the logical intelligence component of the brain. So, in person with level 3 autism, the emotional intelligence component of the brain doesn't work which results in the logical intelligence component of the brain being overpowered. A person with level 3 autism has no way to utilize emotional intelligence. It simply does not exist. This results in the logical part of the brain being far more powerful than someone who doesn't have level 3 autism.

In summation, this means that someone with level 3 autism is a purely logical person. Everything processes through the logical intelligence component of the brain. The senses, the emotions, the speech, all process logically in someone with level 3 autism. This in effect makes them living, breathing, supercomputers. If you can grasp and understand this, it will become apparent why logical inputs and outputs and logical frequencies are so important when someone has level 3 autism.

WHAT THE DOCTORS CAN'T TELL YOU ABOUT LEVEL 3 AUTISM

Because the emotional intelligence component of the brain doesn't work for people with level 3 autism, they have no ability to reason or rationalize. This profoundly impacts the speech, communication and conversations of a person who has level 3 autism. All people with level 3 autism are considered to be nonverbal. Nonverbal doesn't mean that they can't say words. It does mean that they lack the awareness to have direct conversations with people. Most people will find it extremely difficult to effectively communicate with people who have level 3 autism. This is why understanding logical frequencies is so important.

Understanding logical frequencies will give you greater access to someone with level 3 autism. I am convinced that one of these logical frequencies exists within the world of virtual reality. I believe that the logical frequencies that exist in the VR world have great potential to give a parent greater access to their autistic child. That is the entire purpose of the VR LEVEL 3 research study. To give a parent greater access to their autistic child. It is my dream, goal, and mission to make this a reality.

WHAT THE DOCTORS CAN'T TELL YOU ABOUT LEVEL 3 AUTISM

ABOUT THE STUDY

I will explain exactly how VR LEVEL 3 research study works. First the parent will have to provide verification that a medical doctor has diagnosed their child with level 3 autism. I think that the minimum age requirement will be 14 years old. Once verification is established, I will arrange an appointment with the parent/parents to discuss their child's likes and dislikes as well as their strengths and weaknesses. I also want to give the parent/parents a visual of what will be taking place during the study.

This won't be a general or one size fits all approach. My goal is to tailor the appointment as closely as I can to the specific individual. Once the appointment takes place, two Meta Quest 3 VR headsets will be simultaneously placed on the parent and the patient's heads. They won't have to log in or set anything up. When the headsets are placed on their heads, they will be ready to go. The study should take place between the autistic person and whoever has the best line of communication with them. In most cases I assume that this would be the mother. But it could also apply to a father, sibling, grandparent, etc. All study sessions will be monitored, recorded, and videotaped. If there appears to be any dysregulation during the course of the study with the autistic person, the headsets will be removed, and the parent can decide whether they want to continue or stop the session. After the conclusion of the study, I will do an exit interview with the parent to get their opinions and feelings about the study session.

In the beginning phase of the research study, a lot of testing and experimentation will need to be performed as it pertains to the games and applications. This will need to be done to ensure that the appropriate games and applications are being selected for the appropriate individual. Overstimulation and sensory overload are also things that will need to be closely monitored. I will also analyze and review any data that is collected. I will also record videos explaining my findings and observations.

RESEARCH STUDY REQUIREMENTS

These are the things that I will need at a minimum to successfully conduct the VR LEVEL 3 research study:

FOUR META QUEST 3 VR HEADSETS

I will need two Meta Quest 3 VR headsets to conduct one study session. I will also need two additional headsets as backup in case anything happens to the original headsets.

OFFICE SPACE

I will need office space where I am able to conduct the VR LEVEL 3 research study sessions. I need an autism friendly office that parents feel comfortable bringing their autistic children to. I would like to have sensory objects in the office. Maintaining a warm, friendly atmosphere in the office is mandatory.

TWO META QUEST 3 VR HEADSET EXPERTS

I will need two people who understand the Meta Quest 3 VR headsets inside and out. Not only will they need to be familiar with the hardware, but they must also be familiar with the software such as games and applications. They will test various games and applications to verify which games and applications are most suitable for the autistic participants. They will also ensure that the VR headsets are ready to go when they are placed on the parent and child's heads. They will also be responsible for any changes to games and applications that may be needed during the session.

ONE RECORDER

I will need one person to collect, record, and organize any data gathered from the research study sessions. They will be responsible for backing up the data and making sure that it is accessible. They will also be responsible for collecting and maintaining any data obtained from the interview prior to the session. I will need all data to be organized and accessible so that I am able to give my analysis of the data.

ONE SCHEDULER

I will need one person to help me schedule appointments. This person will also serve as my general assistant when they aren't scheduling appointments.

GOALS

If I am given what I need to successfully conduct the VR LEVEL 3 research study, my goal is to get substantial results. My goal is to make the greatest positive impact that has ever been made on the autism community. My goal is to give parents an access to their children with level 3 autism that they didn't think was possible. My goal is to show the world that there is far more to this condition than anyone realized. My goal is to improve communication and quality of life and make the world a better place for persons

WHAT THE DOCTORS CAN'T TELL YOU ABOUT LEVEL 3 AUTISM

with level 3 autism, their families, and their systems of support.

www.ingramcontent.com/pod-product-compliance
Lightning Source LLC
Chambersburg PA
CBHW052115030426
42335CB00025B/2991